Learning Disabilities:

An Astrological Approach

to Successful Living

Dorothy Santangelo

Rex Art Publishing

D1488003

Learning Disabilities:
An Astrological Approach To Successful Living

by Dorothy Santangelo

The author of this book does not dispense any psychological or remedial advice or prescribe any technique as a form of treatment for any perceptual or communication deficiency. The intent of the author is only to offer information of a general nature to help you discern the possibility of the existence of any form of learning disability.

Published and distributed in the United States by:

Rex Art Publishing
655 North Queens Avenue
Lindenhurst, New York 11755

ISBN: 0-9652768-0-5

I wish to dedicate this book with love to...

My son, Jeffrey, whose life prompted me to find the need to write this book;

Dennis Fairchild whose constant support and encouragement forced me to write this book;

Marie Reiss, my friend, my assistant, and my second pair of eyes, without whose help this book would not have come to fruition;

And, especially, to my husband, Robert...

MTYLTT.

Acknowledgment Page

I wish to acknowledge several people and organizations for making this book possible.

Research: Marie Reiss who assisted me in writing this book.

Computers: Dian T. Bustillo whose computer knowledge created the finished product.

Charts: Suzanne Visciani.

Software and Mercury Ephemeris: Matrix and especially Jeff Jawer.

Cover Design: Bev Schilling.

Resource: The Ortin Dyslexia Society

TABLE OF CONTENTS

CHAPTER 1

JEFF'S STORY

Sitting in my office, I ponder just how to put into words the many years of helplessness and frustration my husband, Bob, and I experienced searching for answers to our youngest son's problems. A yellow school bus passes my window and I know in a flash exactly where to begin.

I think back to my tow-headed little boy, eagerly climbing onto that same bus. Excitedly, he looked forward to getting to school every morning. In the afternoons he would shuffle into the house quiet and withdrawn, dragging his school bag behind him. More and more as I looked at his sad, dejected little face, my Cancer mother's heart would break. With this vision strongly etched in my mind, let me go back to the beginning and tell you Jeff's story. Along the way I'll tell you about the search that led me down many paths until I found answers.

After experiencing the adventure of raising my two older boys, Mark and Rob, (I use the word, adventure, because anyone who has brought up a son knows exactly what I mean) by the time Jeff came along I thought I had it down to a science. How wrong I was!

As a baby Jeff was bright and alert, with that wonderful curiosity and eagerness to learn that all toddlers seem to possess. Coupled with that curiosity was a manual dexterity that was astounding for his age. As a tiny tyke he could take complicated pieces of equipment apart and re-assemble them with ease. There was not a toaster, clock or radio that was safe when he was around.

Although Jeff seemed a little slower at recognizing letters and numbers than his brothers had been at his age, he had a phenomenal memory which overshadowed any early indication of a learning problem. He could remember anything he was verbally taught, anyone he had even the fleetest contact with, and was able to give detailed directions to places he had been before. So much so that he became a "back seat driver" in the car saying, "Turn at that next street," or "Go past that white house and then turn," and so on. But, he couldn't seem to learn to print his name or even recognize it for that matter.

My first inkling of a learning problem should have been when he was in a pre-school and we had our first parent/teacher conference. We were told that as long as Jeff was able to accomplish a task or master something new he was a model student. On the other hand, if he was having difficulty, he masked his inability by acting out and being disruptive. At this early age he was already being labeled "hyperactive" and "socially immature," although we didn't find this to be the case at home when he was in his own surroundings. So, as most parents would, we attributed this "immaturity" to his being the baby of the family. Furthermore, since this *was* only pre-school, we didn't put too much stock in their assessment of him and assumed he would outgrow it. Unfortunately, the terms "untrainable" and "psychological problems" began cropping up when he started kindergarten and followed him throughout his years at school.

In the beginning Jeff would eagerly leave for school his usual cheerful self, excited about going and not wanting to miss a day. He would return a different boy; sad, dejected and beginning to show signs of very low self-esteem. It was as if he were two different children; the happy-go-lucky boy in the morning and the quiet, withdrawn one who came home in the afternoon. More and more during those first few years of school we were being told by both his teachers and the school psychologists that, in their opinion, he not only had some type of mental problem, but seemed to be totally "untrainable" as well.

During this time I was finding it increasingly difficult to believe what these "professionals" had to say about my son. Having been a professional astrologer for many years, I decided to approach this problem from a different angle.

Being familiar with the nuances of the planet Mercury and the influence it exerts on our conception and perception of information, I dissected Jeff's chart in every conceivable way, hoping to uncover some underlying factor that might be contributing to his learning problem. Gradually, certain patterns began to emerge. Realizing that I was dealing with professionals who most probably were not open to unorthodox methods of research, I tried, in non-astrological terms, to explain where I thought Jeff's problems might lie, and suggested ways they might easily be overcome. I was labeled "a distraught mother, clutching at straws." Failing to get through to them one way, I tried a different tack, and attempted to explain in astrological terms. Now, *I* was labeled *weird*. No wonder this child had problems!

After years of ill advice and testing by the school system to no avail, we decided to follow up on the diagnosis of "untrainable" and have Jeff tested privately by a pediatric neurologist. Immediately it was determined that his problem was not behavioral or mental as had been suggested all along for so many years. Jeff was diagnosed as a child with a high IQ and a classic case of dyslexia. At last the problem had a name! Unfortunately, we now had to deal with a perceptual problem on top of all the psychological trauma our boy had suffered over the years, but at least we now knew where to begin.

There is, however, a happy ending to Jeff's story. All grown up now and happily married, he is a model maker in his father's factory. When given a picture of something he can duplicate it with ease. Anything that requires assembly, no matter how complicated the instructions, he is able to put together without relying on those instructions. Jeff still has difficulty reading and comprehending complex things. With a lot of patience and hard work on his part, he has managed to overcome his learning disability to a large degree. It is important that a child receives the best help possible at an early age because with maturity, negative experiences with educators often work as a turn-off. This sometimes leads to rejecting any help as an adult. It has been a long, hard battle for all of us, but it is worth it when someone's future is at stake. The astrological insights and information I gleaned from that battle prompted me to write this book. Perhaps it will spare someone else the frustrating search for answers that we went through.

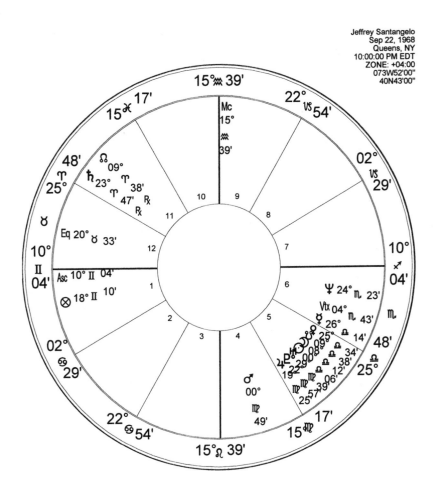

Jeffrey Santangelo
Sep 22, 1968
Queens, NY
10:00:00 PM EDT
ZONE: +04:00
073W52'00"
40N43'00"

15°♒39'

15°♓17'

22°♑54'

48'
25°♈

♌09°
ħ23° ♈
♈38'
♈47' ℞
℞

02°
♑29'

10°
♉

Eq 20° ♉33'

10
9

8

Asc 10° ♊04'
⊗18° ♊10'

11
12

1
2

7
6

10°
♐04'

10°
♊04'

3
4
5

♅24° ♏23'
Vtx 04° ♏43'
☿26°♎14'
09°25° ♎
22°00°09° ♎34'
♇12° ♎38'
19° ♍ ♎12'
♍ ♍06'
♍57°39°
25°

♏

48'
25°♎

02°
♋29'

♂00°
♍49'

22°♋54'

15°♍17'

15°♌39'

©1994 Matrix Software Big Rapids, MI

AFA2 chart style

JEFFREY SANTANGELO
Sunday
Sep 22, 1968
10:00:00 PM
EDT + 4:00
Queens, NY
073W52'00" 40N43'00"

	Crd	Fix	Mut
Fir	1	0	0
Ear	0	0	4
Air	4	1	1
Wat	0	1	0

	Aspect Name	Exact
♂	Conjunction	000°00'
☍	Opposition	180°00'
△	Trine	120°00'
□	Square	090°00'
✳	Sextile	060°00'
∠	Semi-Square	045°00'
ⅴ	Semi-Sextile	030°00'
⊼	Quincunx	150°00'
⅃	Sesquiquadrate	135°00'

Moon in 1st Quarter
New Moon Type
Moon's Motion :
              14°07'54"
Moon is Fast
Sun/Moon Angle:
              008°06'

	☽	☉	☿	♀	♂	♃	♄	♅	♆	♇	☊	MC
☉	♂											
☿		ⅴ										
♀			♂									
♂		ⅴ	✳	✳								
♃												
♄			☍	☍	△							
♅	♂	♂			ⅴ							
♆	∠	✳	ⅴ	ⅴ	□	✳	⊼	✳				
♇		♂		ⅴ		♂	⊼	♂	✳			
☊	☍	☍					☍	⅃				
MC	△	⅃		△			✳	⅃	□	✳		
Asc	△	△	⅃	⅃	□	□	∠			✳	△	

CHAPTER 2

PERCEPTUAL PROBLEMS

Perceptual problems fall into many categories, one of which is dyslexia. Like fingerprints, no two cases of dyslexia are exactly alike. It is a catchall term used to describe the inability to process letters and sounds, resulting in poor reading, writing and spelling skills. Dyslexics often transpose numbers. About 20 percent of the population suffers from some form of dyslexia, with at least half having extreme learning problems.

Unfortunately, most children with dyslexia are not diagnosed until the third grade which is often too late to train them to process words and letters properly. The emotional and social trauma they have suffered by this time is tremendous.

Recently researchers have concluded that this complex trait is genetically linked, since dyslexia tends to run in families. Experts are hoping to isolate the gene and develop tests to identify the disorder before a child even begins to read, and perhaps develop a drug that might help in the treatment of it. Because I had a first-hand experience with this particular form of learning disorder, it led me to seek alternative methods of detecting and understanding it.

People with dyslexia are intelligent individuals who are perceptually handicapped. When they are tested auditorially or psychologically they come up with extremely high IQ scores.

They have problems with right/brain-left/brain function so the message systems in their brains work differently, making it harder to learn or remember, spell or put letters into words. It is my feeling that these are people of the New Age. They have what is called "mixed dominance."

For example, let us say our right brain controls our left eye and the left side of our body and the left brain concerns itself with the right eye and body. In mixed dominance the left brain might also control the left eye and drop down to the right side of the body. This is one thing that has been discovered about dyslexia. Sometimes you might hear of a baseball player who is dyslexic. If you think about the stance of a right-hander, when pitching or batting, in mixed dominance it would be left brain, left eye, right hand, which is a perfect combination for that pitcher or batter.

Additionally, it has been noted that as young children, people with mixed dominance have a tendency to reach for a glass of milk and frequently knock it over. To understand why, try a little experiment. Close your right eye, and reach for a glass of water with your right hand using your left eye to see with. We're accustomed to using the same eye and hand but don't realize it when we're using both eyes. By covering one eye while reaching for a glass, the focal point strays. You'll see it is a little more difficult to reach without spilling.

Dyslexics also have difficulty with letters and sometimes numbers. You'll recognize this trait when a child begins to learn to print and continually confuses the "b" and "d", and "p" and "q". Transposing numbers, seeing the number 24 and processing it mentally as 42, is also a problem many dyslexics seem to have.

Because of perceptual problems, if you ask children with dyslexia to draw a rectangle, often one end will be narrower than the other, but they will see it as even. After looking at the rectangle again they will realize their mistake and correct it. Erasures on homework or drawings in the early grades can sometimes tip you off to a potential learning problem. Many dyslexics are ambidextrous with the ability to write equally as well with both hands. After finally learning to read in the conventional manner, some find it easy read upside-down and/or backwards as well.

Each one of these examples is a different form of dyslexia. In some cases the left and right side of the brain are all connected and there is no right side/left eye dominance. Remember, this is only a perceptual problem. I am giving you these few pointers in order to help you recognize things I was never told to look for while I was dealing with Jeff's frustrating early years.

It is my feeling that many children are coming into our world who have the ability or inclination to integrate the left brain and right brain at birth (or before). In actuality they are probably a little more highly developed than the rest of us. Educators don't know how to deal with them.

Most dyslexic school children are brilliant, but frustrated-- like being color blind in a Technicolor world, or left-handed in a right-handed society. They understand, but can't make words and figures come out exactly right. Embarrassed by these shortcomings, they very often shut themselves off from the world.

It's common for learning institutions to simply categorize children as having "psychological problems." In most cases these poor children become devastated by their feelings of inadequacy, even though they are bright, understand the questions and know answers. Still, nothing comes out as it should. It is like taking an English speaking and reading person such as yourself and dropping you in the middle of urban Russia. Their alphabet doesn't even resemble ours. So here you are, an intelligent person who doesn't speak the language. You cannot understand the alphabet and, therefore, can't read the writing. You can't read enough to get to your hotel, buy something or even read a newspaper. You know you're a smart person, but you cannot even decipher the alphabet enough to find the rest room! That is what it is like for dyslexic children.

As they grow older, many compensate, adapt or grow out of it to some degree but, unfortunately, the psychological damage has already been done. They have gone through a lot of trauma just learning their ABC's. As adults, most of these people get other people to do their paperwork or bookkeeping for them.

Because a dyslexic has difficulty concentrating, often his/her eyes skip over entire lines when reading. The Orton Dyslexia Society works with these disabilities in several different ways. (Information concerning The Orton Dyslexia Society is located in the back of this book.) One of their methods is to use a piece of cardboard with a cut-out slit placed over words and sentences. This enables the reader to concentrate on one word, phrase or sentence at a time.

The Orton Society is now also working with light and color to hold the reader's attention to the line. If you have tutors for your dyslexic child ask them if they know the Orton method. In my opinion it is the best. I believe there is also a grammar school, high school and college for dyslexic people in New England. The Orton Society can give you information about that.

In any grammar school, high school or college, you have every right to have your child educated no matter how difficult the learning disability is. If it is dyslexia, you don't want the child labeled slow, or inadequate, because these are individuals with high IQ's who realize something is wrong with them. A child who does not have a high IQ, or is not as bright as the one at the next desk may not realize he or she is different. They simply get along. They survive, and usually very well. It is OK if their grades are not all A's. However, in most cases, the dyslexic child *understands* that something is wrong, and becomes frustrated. Remember, this is a perceptual problem that has nothing to do with intelligence. If your child is diagnosed with dyslexia you have every right to demand the proper treatment for that child from your school system.

I worked as a child advocate and you would not believe some of the things that go on at the expense of the child. If I had not experienced it first hand, neither would I. The educators want the perfect child to go through the system. They do not want problems, and they do not want waves. Often, the teachers and psychologists have meetings before the parents are called in. An advocate usually sits in to represent the child and fight for him if need be. Many times I have heard remarks such as, "The mother is hysterical, she thinks her child is perfect. Let's just ease things out, and get this conference over with as quickly and as smoothly as possible." Frequently their main concern is about not having problems with the parents or getting sued, rather than with working with the child. Especially if they hadn't recognized early on that the problem was dyslexia. Right now, in their minds they are merely dealing with a disruptive child with psychological problems and hysterical parents. Once the problem is diagnosed, they know what to do. Unfortunately, in many cases classes are so large and schools so under-funded these children sometimes fall through the cracks, so you *must* fight for your child if he has problems.

Perhaps, because learning disabilities were such a major issue in my family life, I began to notice patterns emerging in my astrological practice, as often happens when we are looking for answers. I started to notice diagnosed and undiagnosed learning problems in some of my clients charts. Some were slight and others were much more pronounced.

About this time I was asked to do a reading on a young man we will call Alan, who was an out-patient at a major psychiatric hospital. I was told that he went there for therapy three times a week and might eventually need to be committed. I didn't know why he was coming to see me, I just assumed it was because he had psychological problems. I certainly didn't know he had a reading disability at that time.

Alan was about 22 years old and came from a very good family. His father was a prominent physician. All his life Alan had been sent to the finest schools, and his parents had become increasingly ashamed and disappointed in him when he had not been able to make passing grades. Frustrated, he burst into tears frequently during our reading, when he talked about his failure to do well in school. He said sometimes when reading a sentence or a paragraph he just could not grasp it is meaning. He said, "When I read a paragraph, I know the words but sometimes can't make any sense out of them." He was so upset that I decided to try something. I had one the reading cards I mentioned before that I had used with my son, Jeff.

First I asked him to read a paragraph and he skipped words and lines. He was all over the page. The way he was reading he couldn't possibly comprehend. So I had him read using the card and he thought it was a miracle. Suddenly, he understood what he was reading. I told him I had had personal experiences with reading disabilities and that probably a major part of his inability to comprehend was due to some form of dyslexia.

Of course, by now he had developed many psychological problems due to his learning disability. As I mentioned before, he was a patient at a major mental health facility and, although frequently tested, his dyslexia had never been picked up. Alan took home a cassette recording of the reading with me and evidently brought it to one of his therapy sessions. Not long after, I received a phone call from a therapist at the hospital asking me how I had picked up on Alan's learning problem so quickly. They had been testing him all along for psychological problems (ie., short attention span, hyperactivity, poor social skills) which often mask learning disabilities. Now, after listening to the tape, they had tested him further and he was found to be a classic dyslexic. This poor young man had suffered all those years because his learning disability had not been diagnosed.

The last time I heard from Alan he told me he had a job and seemed, from the gist of the conversation, to be functioning at a fairly decent social level. He said he had made some new friends and had an active social life. Although still in therapy, his sessions were now down to once a week.

CHAPTER 3

UNDERSTANDING MERCURY

Over the years, I've researched Mercury from every angle continually searching for clues to my son's learning disability. Not just as a mother seeking her offspring's "cure", but as a college instructor and professional astrologer seeking "why". Through my work, many sides of this cosmic dyslexic coin became obvious.

I teach Astrology at a community college and my first level students receive every bit of the following information. I have no way of knowing whether they are going to become practicing astrologers. However, if one of them is a teacher or a parent with a child who is having difficulties, perhaps this information may prove useful. It is for this reason I analyze the planet Mercury in every possible way.

Mercury is the planet nearest to the Sun. It is never found more than 28 degrees away from the Sun in either direction. The circle in the glyph symbolizes eternity, infinity, spirit or primal power. The half-circle signifies the soul and the cross signifies the material world. Mercury utilizes all three energies used in the glyph.

Mercury is our communication (mental and physical). It is our urge to acquire knowledge and to communicate it to others. Mercury is concerned with all forms of expression, speaking, gesturing, body language, reading, writing, thinking, drawing, etc.

It also rules day to day travel, channels of transportation, highways, tunnels, veins, arteries, etc.

There are many textbook explanations of Mercury which you are free to research. For this book, I would like to explain Mercury in my own words, dealing only with the facet of Mercury that concerns learning and comprehension.

Since Mercury can never be more than 28 degrees away from the Sun, it can only be in the same sign as your Sun or in the sign before or after your Sun. Mercury rules communications; not just how we think or feel, but everything we are about

For example, let us say you had a frightening experience and you screamed. Someone is creeping up on you, you feel strange. You break into a cold sweat and start to shake. All these things are your body reacting to fright. The scream would be Mercury. In essence, Mercury is the winged messenger that receives and communicates all of your experiences.

Mercury is also influenced by other planets. If I were talking about being in love, for example, and saying something wonderful to someone, Mercury would be communicating the influences of Venus and Mars. And perhaps, Neptune, if I was being poetic. Mercury is like the telephone or loudspeaker for everything else. To see how well this telephone is connected, you have to check its aspects to all the other planets.

For instance, if it is hard for you to express your feelings, desires or anger, your Mercury may have a difficult aspect to the Moon. There may not be a good line of communication sign-wise or aspect-wise to the planet that signifies what you're trying to express.

You also have to check what sign the Mercury is in. Mercury in Aries is a very blunt Mercury--it comes right out with what is on its mind. On the other hand, Mercury in Taurus may be much more laid-back--a much quieter, subtler, Mercury, with a lovely voice, because Taurus is ruled by Venus. Mercury in Gemini is like a mind that is always talking--full of ideas. Mercury in Cancer is very emotional. Each Mercury expresses what the sign it is in indicates.

Let's take a person with Sun in Capricorn and Mercury in Capricorn for example. He would express himself in a very concise, business-like manner. You would know exactly where he was coming from and what was on his mind.

I had two clients who were both Capricorns; one had Mercury in Sagittarius and the other had Mercury in Aquarius. The one with Mercury in Aquarius came in for a reading during which the phone rang and I was told it was a real emergency. As a rule I never interrupt a reading with a phone call but it happened to be my son, away at school, who needed to speak to me (He is a Cancer and I am a Cancer). So I spoke to him for about two or three minutes and told him I would have to call him back because I was in the middle of a reading. I hung up, apologized to the client and told him it had been an important call from my son away at school.

He replied, "If you had done anything else, I would have walked out, because I'm very attached to my own mother. I guess that's my weak spot. I suppose I should disconnect from my mother, but I need a mother. Would you be my mother?"

I said, "Sure."

He said, "Sure, for an hourly fee."

I thought to myself, "There's that Capricorn with Moon in Taurus communicating through Mercury in Aquarius." I knew money would be an issue with him. He really was a very nice man, but it was just the way he put it.

"How would you feel if I started to cry right now?" I asked.

He replied, "Terrible. I wouldn't be able to deal with it."

"Think about what you just said," I replied, wanting him to know that he had hurt my feelings.

A Capricorn Mercury would not have said that, but this was a Capricorn with an Aquarian Mercury--much freer, more disconnected from what he actually meant to say and what he said.

Let us take that same sign, Capricorn. I had a Capricorn student by the name of Patrick, who has a Sagittarius Mercury. Patrick had done volunteer work for our organization.

At one of our functions a member brought her husband, Enzo, with her. Enzo is an Italian from Sicily. Patrick sat down next to him and I could sense what was coming next. There sat the innocent-looking little Capricorn with his Sagittarius sense of humor, and he proceeds to ask Enzo what life is like in Sicily. I thought to myself, "Uh, oh, something's going to happen. Maybe I should leave the room!"

Enzo says, "Oh, it's nice."

Patrick says, "Tell me something. What's the Mafia really like over there?"

Enzo tells him the Mafia is like a fraternal organization of men who get together, socialize, and help each other out with business and family problems.

Patrick looks at him with the straightest face and says, "Kind of like the Knights of Columbus?" That is the Capricorn--

getting the information, getting what he wants--but the Sagittarian Mercury covers up what he is getting at.

When you are looking at a chart, the first thing you should do is see if the person's Mercury is compatible to the Sun, or if it is an "out of sign" Mercury (not in the same sign as the Sun). Basically, the sign on either side of the Sun is really not that compatible.

For example, if you are dealing with an Earth Sun, (Capricorn) you would not expect an Air Mercury (Aquarius) or a Fire Mercury (Sagittarius). Because of the way such a person communicates, people who meet him may not realize that as an Earth sign, he has to be dealt with in very concrete ways. The *Mercury* in Aquarius may express a gift for the abstract but there is a need to see things in black and white because the *Sun* is in Capricorn....and *growth* is through Capricorn. Therefore, Mercury is not the only factor. This person may seem to be quick and have the gift of gab, but we're dealing with a Capricorn, whose ultimate experiences, which enable him to grow, are Earth and practical, not abstract.

The first thing you should to do when you are checking Mercury is to look at the compatibility between Mercury and the Sun. It will only be on either side of the Sun so you won't have to worry about it is being across the chart.

Isn't it amazing that even in astrology you have to deal with your neighbors. You have Venus and Mercury, which travel so close to the Sun, that sometimes you're lucky and have them in the same sign as your Sun. But sometimes, like me, you have Venus or Mercury in a different sign.

I have Venus in Gemini and my desire is to be considered intelligent. But my Mercury is in Cancer with my Sun. So how do I talk? I talk to you like a mother. My greatest need with Venus in Gemini is to be considered smart. With Venus in Gemini I want to be well-spoken. Every time I lectured at a conference people would say, "Oh I love your Brooklyn accent," and I would make a mental note to take a speech class when I got home. I finally did go to a speech class, and I'll share the experience with you.

New Yorkers usually talk through their nose. So the speech teacher asks, "Will the nasal voices please stand up?" and looks at me. I am looking all around because I do not even realize that I talk through my nose. She tells me I have to learn to roll the words over the roof of my mouth. For some reason I cannot seem do that unless I rise up on my toes and enunciate like this, "Helooo, how arrr youuu." So I start practicing my enunciation on everyone.

After taking this course, I was invited to work at another conference. As some of you may know, I have a limited field of vision due to visual problems. So, during the conference I walked around campus saying, "Hellooo," to everyone, and they all replied "Helooo" back.

I tell this story to illustrate the fact that we are all constantly trying to improve our communicative skills. Since this goes on throughout our entire lives, it is important to look deeply into Mercury when reading for adults as well as children.

If there is a Mercury in Gemini the two rulerships tell you that Mercury is terrific in those signs. Mercury in Gemini is very extroverted. Mercury in Virgo, on the other hand, is very introverted. If you're dealing with Mercury ruled signs, you have to take into consideration how they're sending and receiving.

You cannot tell a Virgo that he has the gift of gab and can

say anything he wants. They have the sharpest wit and are very well spoken, but they don't know that, they are very introverted Mercuries. It is very hard to get them to talk. But when they *do* talk, they are *excellent* speakers.

Many comedians are either Virgos or have strong Virgo planets because they are perfectionists. Timing is everything. A joke told one second too soon or too late can fall on its face. Virgos are the masters of precise, exact and perfect. They work very hard at what they do.

Peter Sellers was a Virgo, and he did a skit I will never forget. He spilled some glue on a chair and sat on it. His pants got stuck to the chair. He got up and walked around with the chair attached to him. It was a very silly scene. So stupid, it was ridiculous. But as a Virgo, he did it perfectly, with just the right timing, and it was funny. Comedians can make any scene work if they have strong a Virgo in their charts. If you recall, Peter Sellers was not an outward, stand-up type comic. He was a very subtle, quiet comedian. It is not easy for a Virgo to be a real stand-up comic, but a Gemini would have no problem.

In Peter Sellers' case, he had Virgo rising, with a Sun/Mars in Virgo in the first House. The ruler, Mercury, is conjunct Neptune in Leo in the twelfth house (perfect position for films).

If you have a child, or someone you are dealing with, with Mercury in Virgo, you will have to bear in mind that it is a very *introverted* Mercury. Let us say, for example, you have a Leo child with Mercury in Virgo. Here you are pushing this little Leo to express himself. With Mercury in Virgo, it is difficult for him to do so. This is a *very* important point to remember.

KEY WORDS FOR MERCURY

discriminating　　resourceful　　analytical
brilliant　　　　　aware　　　　　observant
articulate　　　　 expressive　　　refined
dexterous　　　　 versatile　　　　adaptable
precise　　　　　　efficient　　　　scientific
inquisitive　　　　detached　　　　reflective

When poorly aspected or in difficult house or sign positions, I have also seen Mercury expressed the following ways:

unemotional　　unsympathetic　critical
skeptical　　　 indecisive　　　 unstable
argumentative　verbose　　　　worrisome
superiority complex　　　　　　 imitative
over-impressionable　　　　　　restless

CHAPTER 4

UTILIZING THE QUALITIES

The Qualities are also known as Quadruplicities. They are aspects of force. They represent the three basic modes of energy and there are four signs in each division.

CARDINAL   is active, dynamic

FIXED   is stable, sustaining

MUTABLE   is harmonizing, adaptable

MERCURY IN CARDINAL SIGNS:

The key-word is "Activity". Communication is fast, objective, direct and to the point. Mercury is creative because there is an outgoing, driving force. It is also very enterprising.

The Cardinal signs are: ARIES, CANCER, LIBRA and CAPRICORN.

MERCURY IN FIXED SIGNS:

The fixed signs are the most difficult to describe. The key word here is "Will". Mercury communicates consistency and persistence and is non-committal. Fixed signs are the planners and constructors. They never deviate from a set course unless they want to. Being reservoirs of energy and power, they set definite patterns for themselves and resist outer interference . Mercury expresses itself powerfully and forcefully through them.

The Fixed signs are: TAURUS, LEO, SCORPIO and AQUARIUS.

MERCURY IN MUTABLE SIGNS:

The key word is "Flexibility". Communication is easy-going, tolerant and free flowing. Interest is in minute details. Mutable signs are very versatile and therefore must be careful not to scatter their energies. They must be careful of their changeable attitude or lack of persistence.

The Mutable signs are, GEMINI, VIRGO, SAGITTARIUS and PISCES.

Perhaps you can better understand the Quadruplicities if I put it in a story form.

A group of people emigrate to an isolated region. Within the group are Mercuries in every sign. They approach a clearing and the Cardinal Mercuries step forward and announce, "Here is where we will build our city. We will build the hospital and schools to the left, the commercial areas down the center and the fire department and houses of worship to the right. The homes will be built to the north and south of this area."

After this is completed the Fixed Mercuries step in. They dictate the rules and regulations necessary to insure that every · thing will stay in perfect running order. They provide the information needed to maintain the buildings, keep the city's budget balanced and meet the needs of the people. They make sure enough people are instructed to keep the city running efficiently.

Next come the <u>Mutable Mercuries.</u> They institute the changes necessary for the city's progress. They give instructions to move the hospital away from the school so the noise from the playground won't disturb the patients. They have shopping areas built out near the homes to make it easier for people to buy goods. They move the fire department away from the houses of worship and open sub-stations closer to the homes.

Now let us apply this concept to people. Cardinal Mercuries (Aries, Cancer, Libra and Capricorn) like to speak out and be listened to. They like new concepts and ideas. They enjoy a challenge and are very competitive. They like the upper hand in any conversation or debate.

Fixed Mercuries do not like change. They are patient and seldom bored with repetition. They are good listeners and have tremendous perseverance. They like recognition and have good retentive powers.

Mutable Mercuries are versatile, flexible and good conversationalists. They can have varied interests all at the same time. Although appearing to be walking encyclopedias, you may find however, that they have only a passing knowledge of a given subject. They can be very witty but can also be easily distracted or bored.

FIRE	EARTH	AIR	WATER
Aries	Taurus	Gemini	Cancer
Leo	Virgo	Libra	Scorpio
Sagittarius	Capricorn	Aquarius	Pisces

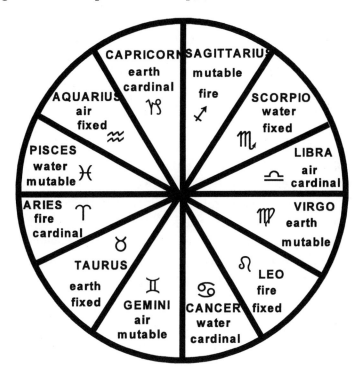

CARDINAL	FIXED	MUTABLE
Aries	Taurus	Gemini
Cancer	Leo	Virgo
Libra	Scorpio	Sagittarius
Capricorn	Aquarius	Pisces

CHAPTER 5

THE ELEMENTS

FIRE:	forceful, enthusiastic
EARTH:	practical, stable
AIR:	conceptual, intellectual
WATER:	emotional, intuitive

The four elements--Fire, Earth, Air and Water--are known as the Triplicities. There are three signs in each division. The elements represent the experiences that the soul attained and brought over into this life to meet the problems presented by the qualities (Cardinal, Fixed, Mutable). These elements form a trine of harmonizing forces of the same nature.

MERCURY IN THE FIRE SIGNS: Represents energy and enthusiasm. It expresses the spiritual side of our nature. Communication is forceful, ardent and extremely impatient.

The Fire signs are:
ARIES, LEO and SAGITTARIUS.

MERCURY IN THE EARTH SIGNS: Is concerned with our physical and material affairs. Communication is practical and stable. Concerns are with our day to day existence.

The Earth signs are:
TAURUS, VIRGO and CAPRICORN.

MERCURY IN THE AIR SIGNS: Communicates on a mental plane to all around. It works through intellect and conceptualization. Air signs are the knowledge seekers. They are creative and highly communicative.

The Air signs are:
GEMINI, LIBRA and AQUARIUS.

MERCURY IN THE WATER SIGNS: Communicates emotionally and intuitively. It is reflective and responsive. Expression is compassionate, passionate and insistent.

The Water signs are:
CANCER, SCORPIO and PISCES

One generally feels secure and confident when communicating through the element their Mercury falls in and somewhat insecure when communicating through the other three elements. If, for example, you have Mercury in a Water sign, it is easy for you to communicate emotions. On the other hand, if you were asked to discuss an abstract concept (usually an Air element) you might find expression difficult. Let me give you an example of Mercury working in different elements.

Mercury in Fire signs has to relate to self. With a Fire Mercury everything is on a personal level. Fire Mercuries talk about themselves all the time. An Aries Mercury has "I-itis", 'I,' 'I,' 'I,' is all you hear out of them.

An Earth Mercury has to be concerned with tangibles; you have to show them an example. They have to see it in black and white. An Air Mercury has a mind taken with ideas and concepts.

The Air Mercuries, the Air planets, the Air Suns, know exactly what I am talking about when I say, "Think about it. Think about this concept."

The Water signs deal very emotionally. They have to relate to how it feels. I am a teacher and I have Mercury in a Water sign. I can only relate and understand through feelings. When I teach my classes, I know I drive the other signs crazy because I make them step into an aspect and feel it.

"Imagine," I say, "what it would be like. Stand in those shoes. Tell me what you would say to this person you are reading when they're feeling like this."

Do not just say, "Oh, you're very cold!" or "It says here you really don't like your father and mother" or something like that. "Step in; see what it feels like not to have a connection with your mother or father because of the aspects. What's it like to feel isolated. It is not that they don't have a connection, they just feel isolated from being able to have a connection." As you can see, with a water Mercury, I can only teach through feeling.

Let us say you have four children and each one has Mercury in a different element. You would be concerned with what kind of teachers they each had. Perhaps one of your children is an Earth Mercury or Earth Sun, (needs to see things in black and white) who has an Air teacher (conceptual, abstract), who never writes things on the board, who just talks and gives ideas and examples. Or you have an Air child (concepts) with an Earth teacher (practical) who bores him to death with documentation. It is not easy to find these things out about a teacher. But when your child comes home and you look at a lesson and you know this child is all Air, you make a story up to teach that lesson. You give him a concept. On the other hand, if you have an Earth child, you have to write that lesson down.

This is not just for children with learning disabilities, this is for any child who is having a problem with learning something. You may have a bright child go into a classroom where the teacher is all one element and the child is an incompatible element. Bored children are usually very bright Air/Mercuries who

28

have Earth/Mercury teachers who do the work on the board over and over again.

Another thing, if your child is so bright that they want to put him in an advanced class where learning is very conceptual, don't put your Earth child in there. He will not do well on a conceptual, abstract level. A Virgo child would be very unhappy in a New Age type of setting where they all sit around in a circle or anywhere they like. Virgos like order, they would want the classroom set up in order.

Someone with Mercury in Virgo must number everything, it must be orderly, like my husband who has four planets in Virgo, and six Earth. People like that must have order. They like everything given to them in order. They like instructions given to them with their work. So you have to see what kind of school system your child is in and how the child is doing in this system. If there is a problem, find out what kind of a teacher he or she has and what kind of educational system it is. I am not saying the teacher or system is good or bad. I am saying it just may be wrong for your child.

Just think, if we could get teachers to understand this, they could break their classes into the four elements and give each group a different approach to learning. This way neither the teacher nor the student would be frustrated. We have a couple of teachers in our group who have done just that. They obtain birth dates from the students' records, have an astrologer look up the Mercury position and place the children in groups according to their Mercury element. They say it is helped them better understand the children's needs.

I am not a Sun sign astrologer, but I have often discussed the connection between Mercury and the Sun. Since Mercury can only be in the sign before, the same as, or after the Sun, you must look at the contact between Mercury and the Sun to see if they are compatible or incompatible. You are here to learn to be your

Sun. If Mercury is the same sign as the Sun, communication is, "What you see is what you get." However, if it is in the sign before or after the Sun, communication is unexpected, so what you see is NOT what you get.

Because Mercury is the planet closest to the Sun there will always be a strong connection between them. There is also a strong Mercury/Moon influence which we will go into later.

CHAPTER 6

MERCURY THROUGH THE ASTROLOGICAL SIGNS

MERCURY IN ARIES: Communicates about self (brags). Welcomes challenges, is argumentative, blunt with the truth, outspoken, prone to exaggeration. An alert, quick-witted, quick thinker, impulsive speech. Can be impatient, have a short attention span, a restless mind, jumps to conclusions.

MERCURY IN TAURUS: Communicates with a practical steady mind, good powers of concentration, a cautious, diplomatic, methodical thinker. Good common sense. Mind on material things. A slow learner with good powers of retention. Deliberate and patient. Fixed opinions, stubborn. Can be opinionated and inflexible.

MERCURY IN GEMINI: Communication is at it is peak, the senses are keen and alert. A restless mind, curious, analytical and logical, needs facts. Is unbiased. A sense of humor, versatile and clever. Can be superficial, have an overtaxed mind, a worrier.

MERCURY IN CANCER: Communication is on an emotional level. Sensitive, psychic, reflective, imaginative and adaptable. A good memory. Is discreet, sympathetic, tolerant and empathetic. Can be impressionable, easily swayed. Communicates strong family ties, could be stuck in the past, have strong anxieties, hold a grudge.

MERCURY IN LEO: Communicates in a dignified, authoritarian manner. Thinks as a leader, sees things in relation to self. Lives in the present. An elaborate vocabulary, dramatic thoughts and words. A creative mind, good concentration, mentally ambitious. Can be pompous, arrogant, have rigidly fixed opinions and feelings of mental superiority.

MERCURY IN VIRGO: Communicates through an analytical mind. A practical thinker, discriminating and well informed, learns easily. Orderly, efficient, a conscientious worker, accuracy and precision are important. Critical, cautious, skeptical, methodical and concerned with details. Can be unsympathetic, unimaginative, always finding fault.

MERCURY IN LIBRA: Harmonious communicator. A good public speaker, is diplomatic, just, considers all sides and compares. An intuitive, creative, refined mind. Appreciates the arts. Charming, social, relates well with others, thinks about relationships. Good at public relations. Can be indecisive, shallow, vain.

MERCURY IN SCORPIO: Brutally frank. A deep, penetrating, perceptive mind, secretive. Hypnotic, sensuous (thinks/talks about sex). Concerned with financial security (thinks/talks about money). Mentally resourceful, shrewd, industrious, determined. Insightful, investigative. Can be vindictive, sarcastic, suspicious, deceptive.

MERCURY IN SAGITTARIUS: Communicates honestly, seeks truth, is tolerant of other opinions, sees the whole picture. Philosophizes, is an independent thinker, prophetic, intuitive, expands ideas. Apt to overlook details, lack of concentration, scattered thoughts, promises too much, procrastinates. Can be blunt, caustic, exaggerate, interrupt others.

MERCURY IN CAPRICORN: Communicates formally. Selects words carefully, is earnest, conventional. A serious thinker, good concentration. A good organizer, disciplined, a methodical planner. Personal ambition, thinks and plans material advancement, cautious, skeptical. Can be too serious, no sense of humor, rigid, suspicious, inhibited expression.

MERCURY IN AQUARIUS: Idealistic, thinks about improving conditions. A good judge of people, objective, intuitive, sociable. Inventive, curious, scientific mind. Thinks for self, studious, interested in anything new, unusual or different, quick to grasp anything new. Can be stubborn, opinionated, forget practical matters and inconsiderate of other people's feelings.

MERCURY IN PISCES: Sensitive, impressionable, imaginative, wants to help others. Good sense of humor. Psychic, takes in others thoughts and feelings, may speak out for those who can't speak for themselves. Subtle, sensitive, artistic, creative, good memory, absorbs knowledge. Can have fears and illusions, emotions could interfere with the thought process, could be illogical, indecisive, withdrawn from reality.

CHAPTER 7

MERCURY THROUGH THE HOUSES

MERCURY IN THE FIRST HOUSE: Intellectually aggressive, mentally and physically active, talkative, investigatory, good reasoning powers. A good writer or lecturer with an adaptable, intelligent and youthful mind. Could jump to conclusions, be impractical, indecisive and think only of self.

MERCURY IN THE SECOND HOUSE: Concerned about money, money making ideas, financial dealings with relatives and neighbors. May have more than one income, talks about money and possessions. Talent in teaching, communication, versatile, adaptable. Acquires education for financial security. Could be impractical, careless with money or have financial problems.

MERCURY IN THE THIRD HOUSE: Talent in areas of communication. Good position for writer, lecturer or teacher. An active, alert and versatile mind. Curious, logical, eager to learn; an experimenter. Thinks and talks about health. Sociable, involved with relatives and neighbors. Involved with short trips (chauffeur, bus driver etc.). Critical, restless mind, could be a worrier. Indecisive, always changing mind.

MERCURY IN THE FOURTH HOUSE: Thinks about personal situation, home and family oriented, home study, may work in the home, handyman in the home. A lot of activity involved with home (people coming and going, relatives or friends visiting or residing), may have two homes. Interest in health and diet. Exploratory. Educational or literary background, mentally active in final years. Concerned with the past or early family conditions. Very emotional. Could have anxieties about home and family, family arguments and problems.

MERCURY IN THE FIFTH HOUSE: Intelligent, creative self-expression. Excellent placement for work in communication, education or entertainment. Good rapport with children, concerned with children's education. Financial gain or loss through investment or speculation. Needs intellectual compatibility in love, analyses love. Mind is on love, sex and creativity. Could be fickle, seek new loves, have an affair with a relative, neighbor or younger person. Dramatic use of words. Thinks and talks about self. Could criticize or worry about children or loved ones.

MERCURY IN THE SIXTH HOUSE: Good communication with co-workers, employers, employees, changes jobs, may have two jobs. Work might include writing or communication. Skilled, intelligent, efficient, concerned with details, knows techniques. Good supervisory or instructional skills. Success and accomplishment are very important. A perfectionist, concerned with details and the practical affairs of life. May travel because of work or health. Can be highly critical, could worry about health or work, or be indecisive about type of work.

MERCURY IN THE SEVENTH HOUSE: Communication with others very important. Very sociable and adaptable with people, involved in intellectual relationships, public contacts. Good negotiator or arbitrator. Good placement for contracts, legal affairs, relationships through correspondence and travel. May write about relationships (personal or work oriented). Could marry a relative, neighbor or someone at work. Possibility of two marriages, more than one partnership, younger partner, an active, clever partner. Could have doubts about relationships, marriage, arguments, divorce.

MERCURY IN THE EIGHTH HOUSE: A deep, penetrating mind, a good researcher or investigator who wants and can get all the answers. Could do research or work with insurance, inheritances, or taxes. A good listener who understands human motivation. Ability to attain desires. Concerned with responsibilities. One whose ideas regenerate others. Spiritual communication. May lecture, write or work in the occult. Death of relative, neighbor, co-worker causes deep anguish, could also result in inheritance. Concerned with inheritance, partner's money (problems could also arise in those areas). Could be secretive or caustic.

MERCURY IN THE NINTH HOUSE: A lover of knowledge, seeker of higher education. An advanced mind with a need to understand. Inspired and idealistic, good at communicating on a religious or metaphysical level. A prophetic dreamer and visionary with a practical philosophy of life. Gain comes through communication, writing, publishing, travel, law, teaching, philosophy. Exploratory. Long journeys involved (mental or physical). Good communication with in-laws. Could be impractical, superficial, opinionated.

MERCURY IN THE TENTH HOUSE: Concerned with reputation, communicates power and prestige. Mind is on achievement and direction in life. Very business minded, education furthers career. Good communication with figures of authority. Makes good use of facts and knowledge, detail oriented, uses foresight, adaptability. Could have two professions, travel professionally, career could involve service and/or communication. Could be deceptive, scheming, become engrossed in trivia, suffer public discredit.

MERCURY IN THE ELEVENTH HOUSE: Mind on wishes hopes and dreams. Original, idealistic, inspired and intuitive. Humanitarian thoughts and ideas. Good placement for counseling, communicating with friends and groups, intellectual friends, younger friends, travel with friends. Socially active with many acquaintances. Friends include relatives, neighbors and co-workers. Could be cynical, impractical, worry about friends and future.

MERCURY IN THE TWELFTH HOUSE: Active, creative imagination. Good communication to an unseen audience (work in television, radio, film, books etc.). Work involves service. Reflective, intuitive a good researcher and investigator. Gain through professional writing, research, psychology, institutions, the occult. Psychic ability. Shy, communication is restrained. Private mind, secret trips, hidden plans, work on secret projects. Could have deep fears, periodic withdrawals, mental delusions, or anxieties over inconsequential things.

MERCURY IN AN INTERCEPTED HOUSE

If you see Mercury placed in an intercepted house in a Natal chart (a house that falls completely within another house), it can mean that this person's expression will be held back regardless of what sign the Mercury is in. Very often the person may be very shy, have a speech impediment, or feel misunderstood. With time Mercury progresses out of the interception and expresses itself better in later life.

To understand the ramifications of an intercepted Mercury, refer back to the chapter on Houses. Review the qualities of the particular house in which Mercury is intercepted. Also, understand that these qualities may not be apparent because the placement of Mercury makes expressing them very challenging.

CHAPTER 8

PERCEPTION
A: THE SPEED OF THE MOON

When the motion of the Moon is fast, our perception is fast.

When the motion of the Moon is slow, our perception is slow.

It is important to check the speed of the Moon. Thirteen degrees, ten minutes (13°10') is the average motion of the Moon. If your Moon is slow, it will be below 13°10'. If it is fast, it will be above 13°10'. The way to find out whether the Moon is fast or slow is to go into the Ephemeris and look at the Moon on the day you were born. 13° 0' is the breaking point; average. Therefore, if when subtracting the zero or noon hour Moon on the day you were born and the zero or noon Moon on the day after, the answer is less than 13°10' the Moon is considered slow. If it is more, it is considered a fast Moon.

Remember, this has nothing to do with the position of the Moon. Just take the Moon position in the Ephemeris the morning of your birth day and the next day and see if it is fast or slow. (For those of you who work with progressions, be sure to check the speed of the progressed Moon and compare it to the speed of the birth Moon.)

Very often people born with a fast Moon go through a period where they say, "I must be losing it, I can't seem to get this." That is because they were used to working with a fast Moon and their Moon, by progression, has moved into slow. This also works the opposite way. Perhaps you needed more time to grasp things and suddenly you find everything becoming easier for you. Your Moon has moved into fast and will stay that way for several years because it is a year for a day in the Ephemeris. When the Moon is moving fast, it does not go fast one day, slow the next. There is an average of three or four days, or more, that it is fast or slow. Progressions represent one year for each day in the Ephemeris, so a slow or fast cycle will be in effect for several years.

Since the Moon rules our perception, a fast Moon has fast perception, a slow Moon has slow perception. You have to think of all the different methods of communication that can be used through Mercury. There are any number of ways we can use to express an idea or concept to someone who is having difficulty understanding. You have to look at the chart to see how they need to perceive it. If they have a slow perception and you are trying to teach them a subject they have to learn fast, you have to realize that a condensed course is not for them. Where the material is verbal; it is not for them. It does not mean they cannot learn it; it just takes them longer to grasp it. If you have a child with a slow Moon whose teacher throws out questions or uses flash cards for math or reading, you have to speak to that teacher and tell them that your child needs a little more time.

You have to fight for these things, otherwise educators think you just want your child to have special attention. A slow Moon cannot comprehend and answer as fast. It has absolutely nothing to do with intelligence, because intelligence doesn't have to do with JUST Mercury.

Let's look at the part of the body Mercury rules. It rules the lungs. Our brain is not in our chest, Mars rules the head. But you wouldn't think of Mars as your communicating planet, even though it rules the head where the brain is. Mercury rules any kind of communication; hand communication, body language.

In addition, it also rules tunnels of transportation. Like your veins, where the blood flows. Short trips, highways, anything to do with movement, have Mercury rulership. So if you are having difficulty with transportation, like going back and forth to work or something short term, you may have a difficult aspect to your Mercury.

One of my students has a problem with dyslexia and has an intercepted Moon. She says as long as she writes things down or takes notes she can remember things but then, at times, she can't decipher her notes. The Moon is your memory bank. The Moon has the best memory of any sign in the Zodiac. She should write everything down but if she's having trouble deciphering her class notes for instance, she should use a tape recorder. Incidently, all learning disabled people have the legal right to record anything.

However, her problem may be a perceptual one since the Moon rules the perception. With the Moon placed in an intercepted house the full potential to perceive the concepts of what you are learning may be held back until later in life. When relaxed, dyslexic people have an unbelievable ability to memorize a well of information and facts.

PERCEPTION
B: SUN/MERCURY POSITION

It is necessary to determine if you have Mercury ahead or behind the Sun. If the Sun crosses the horizon first, this puts Mercury behind the Sun. If Mercury crosses the horizon first, this puts Mercury ahead of the Sun. Your Mercury would be a higher degree or later sign than the Sun if it is behind the Sun and a lower degree or an earlier sign than the Sun if it is ahead of the Sun as the next two diagrams illustrate.

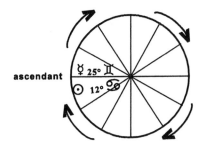

Fig. A: Mercury ahead of the Sun

In chart A, Mercury is rising before the Sun. Although it is in a 12th house position, Mercury crossed the ascendant before the Sun. Therefore, even though it is in the 12th house, and the Sun is in the 1st house, Mercury is ahead of the Sun by 17°.

MERCURY AHEAD OF THE SUN:
THE MIND IS EAGER

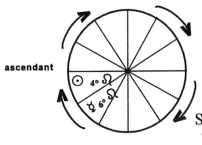

Fig. B: Mercury behind the Sun

In chart B, the Sun will cross the ascendant first, therefore Mercury is behind the Sun. Mercury is coming up behind the Sun by 2°.

MERCURY BEHIND THE SUN:
THE MIND IS DELIBERATE

PERCEPTION
C: COMBINED INFLUENCE OF
SUN, MOON AND MERCURY

1: Mercury next to, or behind the Sun -- Slow Moon
Difficulty in adapting to change

2: Mercury next to, or ahead of the Sun -- Slow Moon
Difficulty in determining priorities

3: Mercury behind the Sun -- Fast Moon
Height of perception

4: Mercury ahead of the Sun -- Fast Moon
Always jumping to conclusions

Mercury next to or ahead of the Sun with a slow Moon--difficulty in determining priorities. Whenever Mercury is ahead of the Sun the person is talking before they see the whole picture. Picture the horizon as the question or the problem. When the Sun crosses the horizon, it sheds light. Then Mercury follows and makes the decision. But when you have to make a decision without the Sun's enlightenment, you're making it without the full picture.

I am often asked if a person with Mercury ahead of the Sun with a fast Moon has a tendency to finish a sentence or answer a question before the other person is finished speaking. Generally this seems to be the case, although that is also a very Virgo trait. Even though Virgos are very quiet, they're ready to move on to the next thing on the agenda. If you find yourself doing this and you have Mercury ahead of the Sun, make sure you've seen the full picture, that you've fully investigated everything before you draw your conclusions or make your answers. With children you have to determine whether their perception is slow or fast and if they are getting the full picture. With Mercury behind the Sun, you know you have the full picture.

For example, take a child who has Mercury <u>ahead</u> of the Sun with a <u>slow</u> Moon (difficulties in determining priorities). If this child's desk is piled high with homework he or she may not comprehend how much work has to be done, what should be finished first, or where to begin. The task may be so overwhelming that you may need to help organize the work. On the other hand, a child with Mercury <u>behind</u> the Sun with a slow Moon, would grasp the situation. The Sun, being first, lights up the whole picture. This child may still need help getting organized but he or she knows how much work there is and will understand the sequence in which it should be done. On the other hand, the child with Mercury behind the Sun with a <u>fast</u> Moon usually wouldn't have any problems like that.

Frequently I have been asked if the combined influence of Sun, Moon and Mercury changes with progressions and if it overrides the Natal Chart positions. The influence does change, however, nothing overrides the Natal position influence. The progressed influence is more like a companion to the Natal influence. Sometimes the Sun and Mercury change positions and the Moon changes speed in a progression. When this happens you will feel the change. But the Natal influence is always the prime influence even though it may feel altered for a time. The Natal Chart represents what we came into this life to learn through or overcome. Progressions are changes within; more spiritual. Unlike transits (the position of the planets on a day-to-day basis), which is like an outer world affecting your chart, progressions are like an inner world affecting your chart. So by progression a person may have a clearer picture or a better understanding of his problem at this time but he still has to go through the learning process to overcome it. The progression may just illuminate it.

CHAPTER 9

MERCURY RETROGRADE
A DIFFERENT MELODY

☿ ℞ About three times a year the planet Mercury (as seen from the Earth) appears to go RETROGRADE in motion, pass through a STATIONARY period, and then assume its DIRECT path again. This illusion is caused by the Earth appearing to be traveling faster on its road than the retrograde planet Mercury.

It has been observed that the various motions of Mercury are largely responsible for unusual slowing down of communications. At this time we encounter confusion, changes of decisions, misprints and misquotes. In addition, we experience transportation and equipment slowdowns, breakdowns, late shipments, lost mail, labor strikes and unresolved negotiations. It is, therefore, wise to wait until Mercury has passed from RETROGRADE through STATIONARY and reassumes its DIRECT motion (up to the degree it held prior to going retrograde), before finalizing any major plans. If, however, Mercury is RETROGRADE in your Natal Chart, this is a good time for you.

This is also a good time for planning, reviewing and for finding lost objects. As a matter of fact, this is a favorable time for undertaking anything beginning in 'RE.' For example: REvising, REviewing, REconsidering, REfinancing, REissuing, etc. Mercury RETROGRADE can be a welcome relief from the daily pace of life. It causes you to slow down and attend to unfinished business.

As you may assume, people born with Mercury retrograde in their Natal Chart usually function very well the three times a year when Mercury is in retrograde motion. Let us talk about a person with Mercury retrograde. He or she may have the height of perception. Everything may appear be wonderful but, lo and behold, they have a Mercury retrograde in their chart. The retrograde Mercury is similar to having a slow Moon. They are not getting the communication in or out properly. So, we are also concerned with the direction of Mercury. If you liken 'Mercury retrograde' and 'Mercury direct' to the slow or fast Moon, you will understand it is not perception as much as the mind's ability to send and receive.

People who have Mercury retrograde receive at a different speed than perhaps the person who is sending to them. They receive and comprehend slower. Consider my husband, for example. He hears what I've said and when I'm in the middle of repeating it, he answers me. The first time he hears something his mind is still processing the information. You think they have not heard, so you repeat it. The second time you have not finished what you were saying and they are answering you. We are talking about a person who sends and receives at a different level.

The three times a year that Mercury is retrograde the rest of us who don't have a retrograde Mercury in our Natal charts experience this, because Mercury is now moving at an incompatible motion to our Natal Mercury. This sending and receiving during Mercury retrograde also works in mundane situations.

Think about the sending and receiving. You do not receive mail, or it is late. (YOU ARE NOT RECEIVING). You don't receive the correct messages at work (YOU ARE NOT RECEIV-

ING). Most times Mercury retrograde, whether in the chart or by transit, is a receiving/sending problem. On a personal level this all boils down to not quite understanding correctly and maybe not being understood correctly.

A child with Mercury retrograde may think he has given the correct answer to a teacher but that answer doesn't come out exactly as the child thinks he is sending it. The teacher who has a direct Mercury is on a different wave length from the Mercury retrograde child. Receiving only what was said, which may be incomplete or incorrect, in the teacher's mind that child is marching to a different drummer, so to speak.

Let us look at another problem for a child with Mercury Retrograde. If the child is doing a written homework assignment, you might be able to spot a problem. Perhaps a word has been left out or changed. He may not know that he is sending the incorrect information and may be marked wrong even though he knows the correct answer but sent it wrong.

This is not about people who have visual problems. We are talking about people with good vision with perceptual problems, because dyslexic people often have 20/20 vision. If you are told your child doesn't seem to see his mistakes, it has nothing to do with his vision. It is his perception. Sometimes dyslexic children have better than perfect vision because the brain is working in both eyes at the same time.

At a number of lectures dealing with the Mercury/dyslexia connection I have been asked if I have any recommendations for a dyslexic person with Mercury Retrograde. For a retrograde I would scrutinize everything they present because, in all probability, you will find they are not communicating information the way they have it in their mind. This does not mean they do not know it; they are just not sending correctly. I would be more concerned with the receiver not having retrograde. You see, two retrogrades understand each other perfectly even if words are left out. For example, people say, "I have Mercury in retrograde, so I don't have to worry about doing things at this time." Let us say they are buying a house. Well, you have to take the real estate agent, the bank, the lawyers and any other entities involved into consideration. They may all have <u>direct</u> Mercuries, so they are in a state of confusion when Mercury is <u>retrograde</u>. With Mercury retrograde in your chart you may feel in control but that doesn't mean everything is going to go along quickly or smoothly. You would have the feeling that no one understands what you're trying to say.

I have also been asked if writing things down helps a person with Mercury retrograde. It may, but remember, if you have retrograde you may not record messages correctly. You may write, "Call Jim," instead of, "Call Jim, immediately!" You are not sending the way you received.

When Mercury retrograde comes into your life through progression it is usually retrograde for twenty-one days because this translates to twenty-one years in a progression. I find that this is often longer than the twenty-one day/twenty-one year cycle. For example, Mercury progressed from 3° of Aries to 12° of Aries and then it retrograded back. You actually function better or clearer when it gets back to that 12° and starts moving forward. While Mercury is in retrograde motion you have to go back and review and revise the decisions made while Mercury was direct.

By progression my Mercury is now retrograde, and it is so ironic that since I became visually handicapped a few years ago, I am now forced to rely on all that I have learned in prior years. When I need something I often recall the information from books

I have read or lectures I have attended may years ago. It is amazing what is stored in the subconscious mind, truly unbelievable. I wouldn't want anyone to lose their sight permanently but everyone should experience it for a short time in order to realize what an incredible file cabinet we have buried in our minds. When I had my sight I never relied on just my memory, so I read new things all the time. When you go into a file cabinet and pull out old files and tapes you find they say the same things over and over.

The one wonderful thing that has happened since I lost my sight is that I have become more aware of what I DO know. I would suggest that instead of purchasing so many books and trying to read so much, you meditate when faced with a challenging situation. You will be amazed at what you have stored in your subconscious mind. You will discover what you know from other lifetimes, and what you have picked up from the universal mind. Things you have picked up from other people, attracted in, and what you have learned through reading and education. Perhaps a natal Mercury retrograde or a progressed Mercury retrograde has this ability but is not always aware of it.

CHAPTER 10

SHORT CIRCUIT
CASIMI and COMBUST

When Mercury conjuncts the Sun within less than ½ degree, Mercury is said to be CASIMI. This means that Mercury is in tune with the Sun. The Solar energy is so well combined with the influence of Mercury that it becomes a perfect carrier frequency for the mind.

When Mercury is conjunct the Sun from a ½ degree to a 4 degree orb, it is said to be COMBUST. This may cause a condition in which the lines of communication are overloaded with Solar energy. I have a combust Mercury in my Natal Chart and when I lecture I have to be careful. I think faster than I speak. I hear every word in my mind but as I speak less words come out of my mouth. When Mercury is combust it seems like an overload. The messages come through so fast you eliminate some words as you speak. That what happens when you have an overloaded Mercury.

There is a new astrological term out now. It is called, "Under the Sunbeams". This is when Mercury is more than 4° from the Sun (combust) but is still within orb of a conjunction to the Sun. Mercury is still under the Sun's influence, hence, "Under the Sunbeams". Mercury receives very good energy from its conjunction to the Sun. This placement works very well except in cases where the Sun is so much more powerful than Mercury that it burns Mercury out (ie., Sun in Aries/Mercury in Pisces).

At one of my lectures I was asked the following question: "If Mars were COMBUST Mercury, would Mars act like the Sun and give Mercury a lot of overloaded energy?" My answer is: Mercury within 4° of Mars is read as a CONJUNCT aspect not as combust. In reading that aspect as a potential for a learning disability, if conjunct, there may be too much anger when expressing, too much energy that may not be released. On the other hand, Mercury may work well combined with all that Mars energy. It could give you a quick-minded, aggressive speaker.

VOID OF COURSE MERCURY

When Mercury is the highest degree planet in a natal chart, it is considered 'void of course'. This term means Mercury will be the last planet that the transiting Moon, as well as other planets, will conjunct before moving on to the next sign.

This Mercury placement causes a person to complete issues in their life by thinking and communicating, often ending circumstances in an argumentative way. Feeling a need to explain things and be understood, they are often known as someone who needs to have the last word.

CHAPTER 11

MERCURY CONJUNCT THE PLANETS
☌ CONJUNCTION: 000°00'

In any conjunction (planets within 7° of each other on either side), you must see if either of the two planets are in signs that are compatible to the expression of the type of energy of both planets. For example, if Mercury CONJUNCT Saturn falls in Gemini, this would be a very good position for Mercury but a difficult one for Saturn. Aspects to any conjunction in the chart can tell you if the power in the conjunction is compatible, positive or negative.

MERCURY CONJUNCT THE SUN:
THE TRUE LEADER

Strong ego. Tendency to talk about self. A powerful speaker and thinker with tremendous mental energy and stamina. Able to communicate ideas well through speech and writing. Quick-witted. Oblivious to self-absorption. (Also refer to the chapter on Mercury Casimi or combust the Sun.)

MERCURY CONJUNCT THE MOON:
THE TRUE REMINISCER

Good sense of humor, very talkative. Expresses feelings with great emotion. A versatile, adaptable, sharp mind. Much thought is devoted to food, family, domestic, and health affairs. An extremely accurate memory with unusual access to subconscious information. Thinks and talks about the past. Hyper-sensitive and moody--highly communicative one minute, silent the next.

MERCURY CONJUNCT VENUS:
THE TRUE POET

Soft spoken. A charming, cultured, well mannered, eloquent speaker. A smooth talker . A lyrical speaking and singing voice. Optimistic nature. Diplomatic, with a need for balance and harmony. Conversation may focus on possessions, money and/or values. Highly communicative to and about loved ones.

MERCURY CONJUNCT MARS:
THE TRUE DEBATER

A sharp mind with boundless mental energy. An aggressive thinker and a blunt speaker. Good at ferreting out information. Loves controversy and can tend to be argumentative. Interrupts others. Often suffers from "Foot in Mouth Disease."

MERCURY CONJUNCT JUPITER:
THE TRUE OPTIMIST

Good mental abilities. Confidence when speaking on higher level subjects (philosophy, religion, law, etc.). An eloquent speaker with a vast vocabulary. Convincing leadership qualities. For the most part extremely truthful. Good language skills; learns foreign languages easily. Very knowledgeable in chosen profession. Can be an incessant talker.

MERCURY CONJUNCT SATURN:
THE TRUE TEACHER

Quiet, often unable to express inner thoughts and ideas but an authoritative speaker in business matters. Very logical, precise and painstaking in speech and thought. Good mental aptitude for math and science. A thorough planner and a serious, hardworking student. Mentally ambitious. A visionary and long range planner. Very traditional in thoughts and ideas. Can be critical and skeptical. A worrier, often subject to fits of depression.

MERCURY CONJUNCT URANUS:
THE TRUE GENIUS

The mind is quick, adaptable and intuitive. This conjunction elevates Mercury to higher thinking and the ability to tap into the higher consciousness. A future planner and thinker. Loves all new forms of communication, especially electronic. An innovative, independent thinker and speaker whose mental concepts are ahead of their time (marches to a different drummer). May appear eccentric at times. Can detach emotionally. The need to do things their way may make them appear conceited.

MERCURY CONJUNCT NEPTUNE:
THE TRUE DREAMER

Extremely inspirational. A deep connection with the subconscious mind often with psychic and telepathic abilities. Interests lie in reading and writing about subjects connected to the mind (psychology, fantasy, mysticism, the occult, etc.). A vivid imagination, can often be deceptive or a role-player. Self-delusionary with a tendency to lose touch with reality. An active subconscious mind that can cause phobias and/or nightmares.

MERCURY CONJUNCT PLUTO:
THE TRUE INVESTIGATOR

A deep, penetrating mind, interested in finding out the how and why of everything. Extremely secretive, often a loner. A slow, steady mind, always working towards change and improvement. Forward looking-- never looks back. A very resourceful thinker. Very analytical and therefore understands the reality in all situations. Can be deceitful and manipulative.

CHAPTER 12

ADDITIONAL ASPECTS TO MERCURY

In the preceding chapter on conjunctions I have listed the energy between Mercury and a planet standing by its side. There is also an influence between Mercury and planets that are placed at various degrees from each other around the chart. Each one of these placements creates a different flow of energy between Mercury and the planet it aspects. Apply the planetary combinations (ie., Mercury/Jupiter) to the aspects written below to see the various changes that occur just by the position of planets in relation to Mercury.

⊻ SEMI-SEXTILE (030°00')
The planets are 30° apart with an orb of 3° to either side. A semi-sextile is a lesson or experience that Mercury can learn from the planet it is aspecting. It is considered a beneficial combination.

∠ SEMI-SQUARE (045°00')
The planets are 45° apart with an orb of 3° to either side. A semi-square is somewhat stressful; more as a feeling of preparedness for an encounter between the planetary energies. This is considered a slightly hard combination.

✳ SEXTILE (060°00')
The planets are 60° apart. I use an orb of 7° to either side. An aspect of great potential and harmony; it is a lucky aspect if ideas are acted upon. It generates great potential. This aspect is considered good.

☐ SQUARE (090°00')
The planets are 90° apart. I use an orb of 7° to either side. This is an aspect of challenge and determination. It can be viewed as an obstacle to overcome or a building block. the encounter must always be faced head-on no matter how difficult the struggle. This is considered a hard aspect.

△ TRINE (120°00')
The planets are 120° apart. I use an orb of 7° to either side. A most important aspect. An easy, creative flow of energy between the two planets; achievements require very little effort. Can cause laziness without a balance of squares or an opposition in the chart. This is considered an easy aspect.

⊡ SESQUIQUADRATE (135°00')
The planets are 135° apart with an orb of 3° to either side. An aspect of provocation, dealing with activity and motivation. A need for endurance or perseverance is necessary to pass the difficulties to reach goal. Feelings of frustration and lack of control are often present. This is considered a slightly hard aspect.

⊼ QUINCUNX (or INCONJUNCT) (150°00')
The planets are 150° apart with an orb of 3° to either side. An inner feeling that something is not right; must pay attention to small details. (Much like the feeling of, "What's wrong with this picture?") Often requires analysis and a quick decision. This is considered a slightly hard aspect.

☍ OPPOSITION (180°00')
The planets are 180° apart. I use an orb of 7° to either side. This is an aspect that must be confronted. Often viewed as the planets

being at odds with each other, it is really an aspect of compromise. This aspect may remain stagnant until one or the other gives way. It presents a strong need for balance and harmony. It is considered a hard aspect.

It is important to remember when reading aspects that Mercury will most likely have a combination of several aspects in a given chart, some hard, some good. These all need to be looked at together. For example: a chart with ☿□♄ (Mercury/Square/Saturn--hard) may somewhat diminish the influence of ☿△☉ in that same chart (Mercury/Trine/Sun--good).

CHAPTER 13

ANALYSIS WORKSHEET

The following worksheet is to be used merely to see how a person perceives and communicates. It is not to be used as a diagnostic tool for the detection of learning disabilities. It is an invaluable insight into the subject's interaction with others, communication skills, perception etc., even when no learning disability is present or suspected.

Fill in the blanks utilizing the information found in the book.

NAME:_____

BIRTH DATE:_____

PLACE OF BIRTH:_____

TIME:_____

Astrological sign for Sun:_____

Astrological sign for Mercury:_____

Sun and Mercury in (select one) same sign   different sign

Influence:_____

_____

Mercury is in the Quality of: (select one) Cardinal Fixed Mutable

Influence:_____

_____

_____

Mercury is in the Element of:
     (select one)   Fire   Earth   Air   Water

Influence:_____

_____

Mercury is in the _____ House.   Intercepted? (yes   no)
Influence:_____
_____
_____

The Moon is: (select one)   Fast   Slow
A: Perception is:_____
_____

B: Mercury is: (select one) ahead of, or behind, the Sun. Influence:____
_____
_____

C: Combined influence of Sun, Moon and Mercury:
_____
_____
_____

Mercury is Retrograde: (select one) yes no
Influence:_____
_____

Mercury is: (select one)   Casimi   Combust
Influence:_____
_____
_____

Mercury is Conjunct the Planet _____
Influence:_____
_____
_____

List additional aspects to Mercury and their influences:
_____
_____
_____
_____
_____
_____

58

CHAPTER 14

CASE HISTORIES

The information in both the text and the case histories is very basic and simple. Often, as we all know, we tend to overlook the basics, which is why much of the information in this book is given at a basic astrology class level. As we progress into more advanced areas such as harmonics, progressions etc., we have a tendency to forget our "Astrological ABC's." I have attempted, therefore, to take advanced applications and make them as easy as possible for everyone to comprehend, regardless of their level of astrological awareness. If the reader considers himself well past the basics, please take the time to read it through. You may rediscover something long-forgotten.

In the following case histories we are primarily concerned with analyzing the planet Mercury. What we are attempting to discover is how these clients are receiving, perceiving and communicating information. This will enable us to explain to the client the best possible way for him to process all his information which, in turn, would be most helpful for the client, teacher or therapist who may be working with him.

For example, if a client has an abundance of Earth in his chart, perception is practical. Information must be in black and white for him. This person is not theoretical and has difficulty dealing with the abstract. In addition, as we look at the charts many psychological, physical or congenital problems may be found. Some may be pre-ordained and some may be directly linked to a learning disability. Our primary concern at this point is merely discovering and offering ways to work with these learning disabilities. In no way am I suggesting that any on-going remedial program or therapy of any kind be stopped. All the case histories studied for this book fall within an IQ range of trainable to high.

CASE HISTORY #1
NELSON ROCKEFELLER

Nelson Rockefeller, Governor of New York State, Nominee for vice-president of the United States, politician, statesman, and grandson of John D. Rockefeller had a learning disability. Not much information is available about his problem. Most books written about him detail his rather austere upbringing which instilled the principles of thrift and public service in the Rockefeller children at an early age.

Young Nelson was a great admirer of his grandfather John D. the first. He was constantly reminded by his father that one of the qualities that made grandfather a success was his perseverance. Old John D. was known for his super-human ability to wait and be patient until he achieved what he set out to do. Throughout his life, Nelson Rockefeller mirrored that sense of achievement.

In the book "I Never Wanted To Be Vice-President Of Anything," authors Michael Kramer and Sam Roberts make mention of young Nelson's dyslexia. They state that Nelson felt that it was aggravated by his father's attempts to cure his "left-handedness." He felt this had a psychological effect on him that further exacerbated his learning problems.

When he was nine years old he was enrolled in the progressive Lincoln School in Manhattan. It was felt personal attention would be given to his tendency to transpose letters and numbers which was considered a "recurring ailment known as dyslexia." In later years it was necessary for him to memorize all of his speeches rather than try to read notes and stumble over his words.

The book also mentions Rockefeller's young daughter Mary asking her brother Rodman why their father never participated in the family's Bible reading sessions, passing when it became his turn to read. Rodman replied, "Because Daddy can't read."

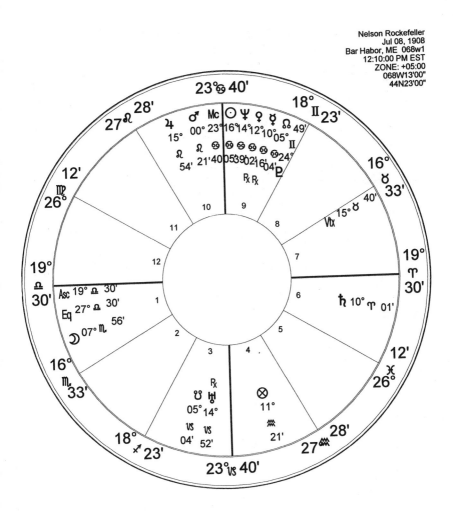

Nelson Rockefeller
Jul 08, 1908
Bar Habor, ME 068w1
12:10:00 PM EST
ZONE: +05:00
068W13'00"
44N23'00"

AFA chart style

©1994 Matrix Software Big Rapids, MI

NELSON ROCKEFELLER
Wednesday
Jul 08, 1908
12:10:00 PM
EST   + 5:00
Bar Harbor, ME
068W13'00"   44N23'00"

	Aspect Name	Exact
☌	Conjunction	000°00'
☍	Opposition	180°00'
△	Trine	120°00'
□	Square	090°00'
✶	Sextile	060°00'
∠	Semi-Square	045°00'
⊻	Semi-Sextile	030°00'
⊼	Quincunx	150°00'
⊡	Sesquiquadrate	135°00'

	Crd	Fix	Mut
Fir	1	2	0
Ear	1	0	0
Air	1	0	1
Wat	5	1	0

Moon in 2nd Quarter
First Quarter Type
Moon's Motion :
        + 13°00'36"
Moon is Slow
Sun/Moon Angle:
        111°51'

	)	☉	☿	♀	♂	♃	♄	♅	♆	♇	☊	MC
☉	△											
☿	△	☌										
♀	△	☌	☌									
♂	□											
♃	□	⊻										
♄	⊼	□	□	□	△	△						
♅	✶	☍	☍	☍		⊼	□					
♆	△	☌	☌	☌		⊻	□	☍				
♇	⊡				✶							
☊	△		☌	☌			□	☍	☌			
MC		☌			☌			☍	☌	⊻		
Asc		□	□	□		✶	☍	□	□	△		□

ANALYSIS WORKSHEET

The following worksheet is to be used merely to see how a person perceives and communicates. It is not to be used as a diagnostic tool for the detection of learning disabilities. It is an invaluable insight into the subject's interaction with others, communication skills, perception etc., even when no learning disability is present or suspected.

Fill in the blanks utilizing the information found in the book.

NAME: _Nelson Rockefeller_

BIRTH DATE: _July 8, 1908_

PLACE OF BIRTH: _Bar Harbor, Maine_

TIME: _12:10 PM EST_

Astrological sign for Sun: _Cancer_

Astrological sign for Mercury: _Cancer_

Sun and Mercury in:

(select one) **same sign** different sign

Influence: _Emotional, Imaginative, Good Memory, Adaptable_

Mercury is in the Quality of: (select one) **Cardinal** Fixed Mutable

Influence: _Creative, to the Point, Enterprising, Driving Force_

Mercury is in the Element of: (select one) Fire Earth Air **Water**

Influence: _Intuitive, Reflective, Responsive, Insistent_

Mercury is in the _9th_ House.   Intercepted? (yes **no**)

Influence: _Interest in Law, Inspired and Idealistic, Good Communication on All Levels, a Visionary_

The Moon is: (select one)   **<u>Fast</u>**   Slow

A: Perception is: *Fast*

B: Mercury is:

  (select one)   **ahead of**,   or   behind,   the Sun.

Influence: *Speaks or Acts Before Having All Information*

C: Combined influence of Sun, Moon and Mercury:

Always Jumping to Conclusions

Mercury is Retrograde: (select one)   **yes**   no

Influence: *Communication Blocked, Often Misunderstood Thinks Differently, Must Review Everything*

Mercury is: (select one)   Casimi   **Combust**

Influence: *Overload, Thinks Faster than Can Express*

Mercury is conjunct the Planet(s) *Sun, Venus, Neptune*

Influence: *Mercury/Conjunct/Venus: Eloquent Speaker Diplomatic Mercury/Conjunct/Neptune: Inspirational, Vivid Imagination, A Roleplayer (Deceptive). Mercury/Conjunct/Sun: Powerful Speaker and Thinker with Tremendous Mental Energy and Stamina*

List additional aspects to Mercury and their influences:

Mercury and the Three Conjunctions Oppose Uranus, Causing a Compromise Between Tradition and Innovation, Commitment and Independence. Often Struggling with Concepts Ahead of their Time. Mercury/Square/Saturn: Precise and Painstaking in Speech and Thought. Authoritative, Often Unable to Express Inner Thoughts.

BRIEF SUMMARY OF WORKSHEET:
NELSON ROCKEFELLER

Nelson Rockefeller was known to be a dyslexic who, despite his learning disability, went on to have a successful political career. His chart indicates a person whose mind works very well. He has Mercury and the Sun in Cancer; Cancer works a lot on feelings and intuition. His Moon (Scorpio) also indicates he is very perceptive.

With Mercury retrograde, this is a person who would have to have his work reviewed and corrected. He would often feel that people didn't understand what he was trying to communicate. While discussing one thing, his mind was probably wandering to several other topics. The best way for him to learn and communicate would be through structure (Mercury/Square/Saturn). His teachers would have had to be innovative to be able to hold his attention (Mercury/Opposing /Uranus) (Neptune/Conjunct/Sun). This was a person who learned more by observation and practical application than by books. Any training for him would have had to be "hands on," fast moving, using the latest methods or aids. His charm and charisma (the conjunctions to Mercury) would have made people like him, and also would have made him very persuasive.

The chart indicates an exceptionally good communicator which would have helped in overcoming a learning disability. Being a very high achiever, he was able to mask many of his shortcomings in those areas. He felt a tremendous responsibility to achieve any task he took on. With this strong sense of responsibility, regardless of his affluent circumstances, he would have succeeded in any endeavor he undertook.

With Mercury and its conjunctions all in the ninth house, there would have been a strong desire for higher education. Mercury opposing Uranus in the third house would indicate many changes in schools and/ or teachers before the solution to his problem was found.

CASE HISTORY #2
GENERAL GEORGE S. PATTON

George Smith Patton, Jr. was one of the world's greatest army commanders. Distinguished as an inspiring battlefield leader, with his discipline, determination and proficiency in troop deployment; he had few equals in the areas of strategy and theory and has been called the greatest combat general of modern times.

Coming from a long line of distinguished military men who were graduates of West Point and VMI, he had been inspired by them as a child, and determined to follow in their footsteps. By the end of his military career he had far surpassed them on the field of battle. He was also severely dyslexic.

As a child it soon became apparent that young George was extremely intelligent but was experiencing difficulties learning to read and write. Rather than have him suffer the taunts of the other children at school, his parents hired tutors for him and they, themselves, also devoted a tremendous amount of time teaching him. By age eleven he had learned to read and write sufficiently and was sent to a private school where he remained enrolled until the age of eighteen. Up to that time, he still had problems with written tests and in order for him to score highly, had to be tested orally.

Through his father's influence, he won an appointment to West Point, but was unable to pass the written entrance exams. Undaunted, his father got him accepted to his alma mater, Virginia Military Institute. George distinguished himself there as a first year cadet, and re-applied to West Point the following year. Through diligence and determination he was able to pass the exams and went on to begin his military career.

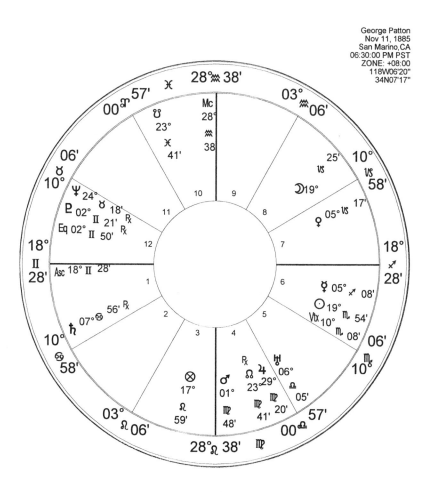

George Patton
Nov 11, 1885
San Marino, CA
06:30:00 PM PST
ZONE: +08:00
118W06'20"
34N07'17"

©1994 Matrix Software Big Rapids, MI

AFA chart style

	Aspect Name	Exact
☌	Conjunction	000°00'
☍	Opposition	180°00'
△	Trine	120°00'
□	Square	090°00'
✶	Sextile	060°00'
∠	Semi-Square	045°00'
⊻	Semi-Sextile	030°00'
⊼	Quincunx	150°00'
⊡	Sesquiquadrate	135°00'

	Crd	Fix	Mut
Fir	0	0	1
Ear	2	1	2
Air	1	1	2
Wat	1	1	0

Moon in 1st Quarter
Crescent Type
Moon's Motion :
    11°54'11"
Moon is Slow
Sun/Moon Angle:
    59°31'

	☽	☉	☿	♀	♂	♃	♄	♅	♆	♇	☊	MC
☉	✶											
☿	∠											
♀		∠	⊻									
♂	⊡		□	△								
♃	△	✶	✶	□	⊻							
♄		⊡	⊼	☍	✶	□						
♅		∠	✶	□		☌	□					
♆	△	☍			□	△	∠					
♇	⊡		☍	⊼	□	△		△	☌			
☊	△	✶			☌			△	△			
MC		□	□	✶	☍	⊼	△		□	□		
Asc	⊼	⊼									□	

71

ANALYSIS WORKSHEET

The following worksheet is to be used merely to see how a person perceives and communicates. It is not to be used as a diagnostic tool for the detection of learning disabilities. It is an invaluable insight into the subject's interaction with others, communication skills, perception etc., even when no learning disability is present or suspected.

Fill in the blanks utilizing the information found in the book.

NAME: *George S. Patton*

BIRTH DATE: *November 11, 1885*

PLACE OF BIRTH: *San Marino, California*

TIME: *6:30 PM PST*

Astrological sign for Sun: *Scorpio*

Astrological sign for Mercury: *Sagittarius*

Sun and Mercury in (select one)   same sign   **different sign**

Influence: *Independent Thinker, Intuitive Prophetic: Seeks Truth, Expansive Thinker, Can Be Blunt and Caustic.*

Mercury is in the Quality of:

(select one)   Cardinal   Fixed   **Mutable**

Influence: *Interested in Minute Details, Very Versatile*

Mercury is in the Element of:

(select one) **Fire**   Earth   Air   Water

Influence:*Communication Is Forceful, Ardent, and Extremely Impatient. Tremendous Enthusiasm*

Mercury is in the __6th__ House.   Intercepted? (yes **no**)

Influence: *Good Rapport with Employees (Troops) Good Supervisor, Skilled, Intelligent, Efficient Concerned With Details, Success and Accomplishment Very Important*

The Moon is: (select one)   Fast   **Slow**

A: Perception Is: *Slow*

B: Mercury is: (select one) ahead of, or **behind,** the Sun.

Influence: *Deliberate Mind*

C: Combined influence of Sun, Moon and Mercury:

Difficulties in Adapting to Change

Mercury is Retrograde: (select one) yes **no**

Influence:

Mercury is: (select one)   Casimi   Combust

Influence:

Mercury is Conjunct the Planet _____
Influence:_____

_____

List additional aspects to Mercury and their influences:

Mercury/Semi-Sextile/Venus: Many Lessons Learning to Communicate to and about Loved Ones. Need to Learn Diplomacy. Need To Be Optimistic. Mercury/Sextile/Jupiter: Potential for Leadership Qualities, Learning Languages, Extremely Truthful, Knowledgeable in Chosen Profession. Can Be an Expansive Talker. Mercury/Sextile/Uranus: Potential for Quick, Adaptable, Intuitive Mind, a Future Planner with Ability to Tap into Higher Consciousness. Mercury/Square/Venus: Manner of Speech Blunt, Argumentative. Mind Has Tremendous Energy, Interrupts. Many Mental Obstacles to Overcome. Strong Mental Determination. Mercury/Quincunx/Saturn: Authority and Mental Responsibility. Use of "Gut Feelings" When Planning His Battles. Very Good at Analysis, with Attention to Small Details. Able to Make Quick Decisions. Mercury/Opposing/Pluto. Necessity to Compromise the Energy of These Two Planets. Seeks Balance, but Often Gives In to One or the Other of the Two Planets. Secretive, a Loner. A Slow, Analytical Thinker. Must Often Follow Psychic, Subconscious Intuition When Making Decisions. Pluto Is the Ruler of His Sun.

SUMMARY OF WORKSHEET
GEORGE S. PATTON

I would like to state at the outset that George Patton had a 19°54' Scorpio Sun, which falls on a degree known as "Serpentine." This degree empowered him with the ability to make people follow him anywhere. It is considered a degree of leadership.

Mercury in the sign of Sagittarius made him appear jovial and carefree, even though he is an extremely serious and private person. Mercury in the Sixth House indicates that part of his daily tasks during his life would be concerned with communication and mental pursuits. This placement also endowed him with the ability to have a good rapport with subordinates, making him a strong leader throughout his life and career.

With regard to the two Sextiles, he was very lucky especially with Mercury in Sagittarius sextiling its own ruler, Jupiter. Jupiter is his void of course planet, so all his mental pursuits were taken to their completion. The Moon is slow, indicating slow perception, but the Moon makes an exact sextile to the Sun which gives it added energy.

Mercury/Square/Mars could often make him angry and rash, causing him to be his own worst enemy at times. Mercury/Quincunx/Saturn was probably one of his best assets. It enabled him to feel very responsible about checking into details that might be a stumbling block to the completion of his goals, or personally assigned tasks.

In all probability the single most important aspect in his chart was Mercury opposing Pluto in two mutable signs, both of which deal with great mental pursuits. Although he was a private person, with Mercury in a fire sign, he had to be true to himself, and needed to be honest in expressing himself about what he believed to be right. Most likely he was a very serious child with an optimistic attitude, strong mental drive and powerful intuitive energy. These assets enabled him to overcome his learning disability.

CASE HISTORY #3
JOE CRINITA

Joey Crinita is one of Canada's foremost spiritualist mediums. He is well known for his lectures, books, spiritual counseling and healing. Although a lover of words and an avid reader today, as a child, growing up in a large Montreal family, he had numerous problems in school.

He states that it was very difficult for him to learn to read due to a tendency to transpose letters and numbers, which is one of the classic indicators of dyslexia. To this day, he says he still has difficulty reading, having to go back over a page or paragraph which makes no sense to him because he has skipped over a word or sentence the first time. He has always found it much easier to learn new words by hearing them pronounced and spelled, rather than by reading them. Conventional methods of learning were never easy for him, consequently, although he was a good student, he became easily bored.

He did, however, learn as most dyslexics do, to compensate. If something caught his interest, once he learned it, he never forgot it. This aspect of his personality has carried over into his adult life, making him a very well versed and knowledgeable individual.

Joey stated he found it very difficult grasping the concepts of mathematics. Because he has difficulty solving mathematical problems in the conventional way, he is able to come up with the right answers in his own way. Again, transposing numbers proved to be a stumbling block for him. He still has this problem and finds he frequently mixes up telephone numbers when writing them down.

Not possessing the manual dexterity that some dyslexics have, Joey does not use either a typewriter or personal computer when writing his books and lectures, preferring to do everything in longhand.

He says he has always had problems with directions, (ie. left and right, north, east, south and west) and finds he must make a concerted effort to discern which is which. Because of this confusion, it is very difficult for him to read maps and/or follow directions. Therefore, although he has a license, he finds driving an automobile makes him very uneasy and prefers not to if possible.

Joey says the inability to determine left from right may be a fairly common trait among people who are psychic, since he knows other mediums with this problem. Perhaps this may have something to do with both sides of the brain operating at the same time, which could be a clue to psychic ability or channeling.

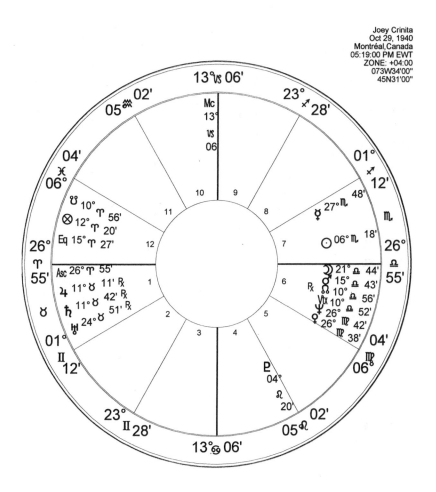

Joey Crinita
Oct 29, 1940
Montréal, Canada
05:19:00 PM EWT
ZONE: +04:00
073W34'00"
45N31'00"

AFA chart style

JOEY CRINITA
Tuesday
October 29, 1940
5:19:00 PM
EWT   + 4:00
Montreal, QU
073W34'00"   45N31"00"

	Aspect Name	Exact
☌	Conjunction	000°00'
☍	Opposition	180°00'
△	Trine	120°00'
□	Square	090°00'
✶	Sextile	060°00'
∠	Semi-Square	045°00'
ⅴ	Semi-Sextile	030°00'
⊼	Quincunx	150°00'
⚼	Sesquiquadrate	135°00'

	Crd	Fix	Mut
Fir	1	1	0
Ear	1	3	2
Air	2	0	0
Wat	0	2	0

Moon in 4th Quarter
Balsamic Moon Typ
Moon's Motion :
        + 15°08'00"
Moon is Fast:
Sun/Moon Angle:
        345°25'

	☽	☉	☿	♀	♂	♃	♄	♅	♆	♇	☊	MC
☉												
☿												
♀			✶									
♂	☌		∠									
♃		☍	⚼									
♄		☍	⚼		☌							
♅	⊼		☍	△								
♆			✶	☌	⚼	⚼	△					
♇		□	△	✶	□	□	✶	✶				
☊			∠		☌	⊼	⊼	⚼		✶		
MC	□	✶	∠		□	△	△			□		
Asc	☍	☍	⊼	⊼					ⅴ	⊼	□	

ANALYSIS WORKSHEET

The following worksheet is to be used merely to see how a person perceives and communicates. It is not to be used as a diagnostic tool for the detection of learning disabilities. It is an invaluable insight into the subject's interaction with others, communication skills, perception etc., even when no learning disability is present or suspected.

Fill in the blanks utilizing the information found in the book.

NAME: _Joey Crinita_

BIRTH DATE: _October 29, 1940_

PLACE OF BIRTH: _Montreal, Quebec, Canada_

TIME: _5:19 PM EDT_

Astrological sign for Sun: _Scorpio_

Astrological sign for Mercury: _Scorpio_

Sun and Mercury in (select one) **same sign** different sign

Influence: _Deep, Penetrating, Perceptive Mind. Mentally Resourceful; Insightful, Shrewd and Industrious; Hypnotic, Secretive_

Mercury is in the Quality of:

(select one) Cardinal **Fixed** Mutable

Influence: _Powerful, Forceful Expression, Consistent and Persistent, Never Deviating from Set Goals; Resistant to_

Outside Influence

Mercury is in the Element of:

(select one) Fire Earth Air **Water**

Influence: *Communication Is Emotional and Intuitive, Reflective and Responsive; Expression Is Passionate, Compassionate and Insistent*

Mercury is in the **7th** House.   Intercepted? (**yes** no)

Influence: *Communication in Expression Is Held Back; Delay in Partnerships or Relationships*

The Moon is: (select one)   **Fast** Slow

A: Perception is: *Extremely Fast Perception (Speed - 15:08)*

B: Mercury is: (select one) ahead of, or **behind,** the Sun.

Influence: *Mind Is Deliberate*

C: Combined influence of Sun, Moon and Mercury:

Height of Perception

Mercury is Retrograde: (select one) yes **no**

Influence:

Mercury is: (select one)   Casimi   Combust

Influence:_____

_____

Mercury is Conjunct the Planet _____

Influence:_____

_____

List additional aspects to Mercury and their influences:

Mercury/Sextile/Venus: Very Good, Soft Speaking Voice;
Relaxed. Mercury/Sextile/Neptune: Intuitive, Perceptive,
Good Memory, Strong Connection to the Subconscious. Mer-
cury/semi-square/mars: Ambitious, Frequently Challenged.
Conflict in Communication; Frustration; Impulsive Speech
at Times. Stress/tension. Mercury/Trine/Pluto: Mercury in
Scorpio/Trine/Pluto (Ruler of Scorpio) Charismatic, Creative,
Humorous. Good at Research, Able to Make Change, a Deep
Thinker. Mercury/Opposing/Uranus: Cooperation Is Nec-
essary, Mental Struggle, Often Misunderstood; Confronta-
tional. A Unique Thinker and Speaker

_____

_____

_____

_____

_____

_____

SUMMARY OF WORK SHEET:
JOEY CRINITA

Joey Crinita graciously agreed to be a case study for this book. I'm sure many of you have had the opportunity to read his books or hear him lecture. Few have had the privilege of knowing the man as I have and to understand the internal struggle he underwent to achieve his many accomplishments.

In my long standing relationship with Joey I have always sensed an underlying lack of confidence. I found this to be puzzling given the fact that he is extremely knowledgeable in so many areas. After analyzing his chart for this project, I now have a clearer picture of this paradox.

His chart is a good example of one that, at first glance, doesn't have a significant amount of information dealing with a learning disability. Once knowing the subject and on closer observance, the answers begin to materialize in the chart.

Initially, I attributed some of his insecurities to the fact that he had an interrupted formal education. However, the more I got to know him, the more I realized how well versed he is on any number of subjects that hold his interest. In correspondence, I found his writing to be both humorous and deep. His ability to cover up almost anything is quite typical of the Scorpio nature, therefore he will sometimes resort to wry humor to mask his true feelings.

His Sun and Mercury are in the same sign which makes him very straight forward. With him it is, " What you see, is what you get." With his Mercury in a Fixed sign, he sticks to a task or goal until he masters it. However, as was mentioned earlier, although he is a prolific lecturer and writer he has never been able to cope with the mastery of the typewriter, word processor or PC, and writes everything by hand.

Mercury in a Water sign makes him extremely emotional and intuitive. Good intuition is beneficial to a person with a learning disability because they sometimes assimilate information on a more subconscious level. With the intercepted Mercury in the seventh house he would have the tendency to view others as more intelligent than himself, thereby holding back and not expressing his own opinions until later in life. This would also tend to cause him to avoid confrontations with others, making him back away whether or not he felt he was right, while mulling it over in his mind.

Joey has a Mercury/Sextile/Venus which makes him a soft spoken romantic. This aspect was my first clue to his deeper nature. Often while on long walks or trips together we would get into some very deep conversations and at times when words failed him, he would resort to song. Sometimes a love song, sometimes a funny song, and sometimes a very sad song. At other times he would become "The Great Impersonator," expressing himself through the voice of Ghandi or some other well known celebrity.

Mercury/Sextile/Neptune gives him an extremely good memory and excellent perceptive abilities which tie into his mediumship.

The aspect of Mercury/Semi-Square/Mars indicates his anger would be expressed verbally rather than physically. This aspect also makes him hold on to his anger and verbalize it long after it should have been forgotten.

His Mercury is trine Pluto and although this trine is beneficial, giving him charisma and a sense of humor, note that it is not in the same element, and both planets are in fixed signs. This tends to make him more stubborn about changes and new things entering his life. Since Pluto is in the sign of Leo, when he does activate anything new or different in his life, he has to be certain that he will appear in a good light and never, ever, be embarrassed.

In the Mercury/Uranus opposition you would most likely see where most of his learning problems lie. Since Mercury, our planet of communication, and Uranus, its higher octave, are both in intercepted houses, its easy to see how processing information would be difficult for Joey. Even though he tended to have a different thinking process as a child due to Uranus being in the first house, he always would have felt that whatever others told him was more correct, because Mercury was in the seventh house. This was the cause of a great mental struggle for him throughout his life.

With Uranus in the first house he could very easily lapse into imitations of celebrities as a means of expressing himself or to defuse a situation. This is probably what helped him get through his early school years.

In his interview Joey discussed his inability to discern left from right and the transposing of numbers and letters. These are classic symptoms of dyslexia, and indicate the integral use of both sides of the brain at the same time. Perhaps this contributes to making him one of the most talented mediums of our time.

The following two case histories give credence to the theory that dyslexia is hereditary. This theory has just recently been proven a fact and links dyslexia and related disabilities to a genetic factor. Regrettably, the third member of the family mentioned, would not give permission for the use of his chart and analysis.

CASE HISTORY #4:
MALE, JULY 3, 1919

As a child, in grammar school, he had a very difficult time learning to read and write. Having lost his mother at a very early age, the nuns in the parochial school he attended looked at his learning disability as a behavioral problem, since dyslexia was not widely known in those days. Consequently, he was disciplined regularly for a situation he had no control of.

After being called to school on a number of occasions, the subject's father wisely decided that it would be better for the child if he attended public school. Out of an atmosphere where he felt pressured, the boy started to blossom. With the help of a very caring, patient third grade teacher, he began to overcome his learning problems. He did well academically in high school although, he always needed to have all the details in order to fully understand a concept or situation. This need for details carried over into his adult life.

While in high school he participated in student plays and operettas and played championship football. Although he was unable to afford to go to college, he was self-taught. He had a brilliant mind and a tremendous thirst for knowledge throughout his life.

Despite his early learning disability, this man was able to overcome it and go on to become a very successful businessman who was highly respected in his field. He founded the first credit union in the New York Greyhound Transportation system and served as its first president. When Greyhound went into the package express business, he was asked to head up that department, which he did, for a number of years. Upon leaving Greyhound, he went into his own freight forwarding business, where he was involved in the transportation of government personnel household goods. Elected president of an international freight forwarders association, he served for a number of years before his retirement.

After retirement he bought one of the first personal computers on the market and taught himself to become a very proficient user. He was a volunteer guide in a local museum, taught a defensive driving course and served as one of the first arbitrators for the New York State Automobile Lemon Law. Being a senior citizen, he became involved with the Nassau County Department of Senior Affairs and counseled seniors on Medicare. He also managed to attend college part-time. Throughout his life, this man never allowed his early learning disability to stand in his way.

His older daughter, although a bright child, also had problems in grammar school, and was referred to as "inattentive," "uncooperative" and "a behavior problem" by her second and third grade teachers. The subject attributed this to "like father, like daughter" and felt she would outgrow it just as he had.

His second child, a son, was having problems learning to

read and write some ten years later and through testing was finally diagnosed as being dyslexic, after having repeated the second grade. When the subject learned what the indicators were concerning that diagnosis, he realized that these were some of the same problems he had experienced as a child in school.

In discussing this with his daughter, who was eleven years older than her brother, they realized that they both had suffered from undiagnosed dyslexia as children and all three of them had been around the same age and same grade level when the learning problem was most prevalent.

Fortunately, father and daughter had been able to learn to compensate and eventually overcome it for the most part, without the benefit of remedial training. Although, in both cases the subjects stated that as adults, they still occasionally have problems with the transposition of letters and numbers.

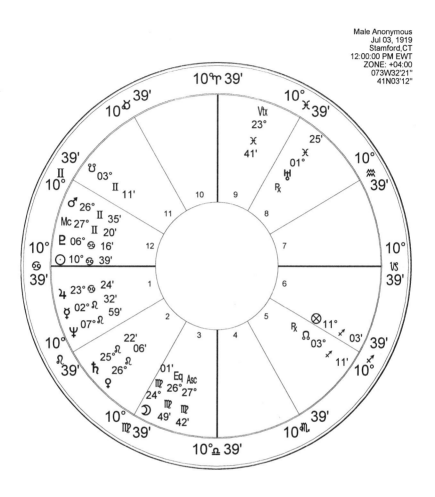

Male Anonymous
Jul 03, 1919
Stamford, CT
12:00:00 PM EWT
ZONE: +04:00
073W32'21"
41N03'12"

90

AFA2 chart style

	Aspect Name	Exact
☌	Conjunction	000°00'
☍	Opposition	180°00'
△	Trine	120°00'
□	Square	090°00'
✶	Sextile	060°00'
∠	Semi-Square	045°00'
ⅴ	Semi-Sextile	030°00'
⊼	Quincunx	150°00'
⊡	Sesquiquadrate	135°00'

MALE
Thursday
Jul 3, 1919
00:00:00 PM
EWT + 4:00
Stamford, CT
073W32'00"   41N03"00"

	Crd	Fix	Mut
Fir	0	4	0
Ear	0	0	2
Air	0	0	2
Wat	3	0	1

Moon in 1st Quarter
Crescent Type
Moon's Motion :
         + 12°29'39"
Moon is Fast
Sun/Moon Angle:
         73°21'

	D	☉	☿	♀	♂	♃	♄	♅	♆	P	☊	MC
☉												
☿	✶											
♀	ⅴ	∠										
♂	□		✶									
♃	✶		☌	ⅴ								
♄	ⅴ	∠		☌	✶	ⅴ						
♅		△	⊼	☍	△		☍					
♆	∠	ⅴ	☌									
P		☌			☌			△	ⅴ			
☊	✶		△	□		△	□	□	△			
MC	□			✶	☌		✶	△		☌		
Asc	☌		✶	ⅴ	□	✶	ⅴ			□	✶	□

91

ANALYSIS WORKSHEET

The following worksheet is to be used merely to see how a person perceives and communicates. It is not to be used as a diagnostic tool for the detection of learning disabilities. It is an invaluable insight into the subject's interaction with others, communication skills, perception etc., even when no learning disability is present or suspected.

Fill in the blanks utilizing the information found in the book.

NAME: *Male*

BIRTH DATE: *July 3, 1919*

PLACE OF BIRTH: *Stamford, Connecticut*

TIME: *Unknown*

Astrological sign for Sun: *Cancer*

Astrological sign for Mercury: *Leo*

Sun and Mercury in (select one)   same sign   <u>different sign</u>

Influence: *Sees Things in Relation to Self (Leo) Rather than on an Emotional Level (Cancer). Elaborate Vocabulary, Mentally Ambitious with Good Concentration. Feels Mentally Superior*

Mercury is in the Quality of:

(select one) Cardinal **Fixed** Mutable

Influence: *Strong-Willed and Persistent, Sets Definite for Himself, Resisting Outer Interference*

Mercury is in the Element of: (select one) <u>Fire</u> Earth Air Water

Influence: ***Extremely Impatient with Self, But Very Enthusiastic to Learn, Very Forceful in Communication***

(unknown)

Mercury is in the *(solar chart)* House. Intercepted? (yes no)

Influence:_____

The Moon is: (select one)   Fast **Slow**

A: Perception is: ***Slow***_____

B: Mercury is: (select one) ahead of, or <u>behind</u>, the Sun.

Influence: ***The Mine Is Deliberate***_____

C: Combined influence of Sun, Moon and Mercury:

Difficulty in Adapting to Change, Weigh Words, Thinks Before Speaking_____

Mercury is Retrograde: (select one) yes   **<u>no</u>**

Influence:_____

Mercury is: (select one)   Casimi   Combust

Influence:_____

Mercury is Conjunct the Planet _**Wide Conjunction to Jupiter and**_
**Conjunct Neptune**

Influence: _**Mercury/Conjunct/Jupiter: Good Mental Abilities, Elo-**_
**quent Speaker, Vast Vocabulary, Incessant Talker Mercury/Con-**
**junct/Neptune: Intuitive Vivid Imagination. Interested in Subjects**
**Connected to the Mind. Can Be Self-Deceptive, Self-Delusionary**

List additional aspects to Mercury and their influences:

**Mercury/Sextile/Moon: Very Emotional About New Ideas or Con-**
**cepts, Able to Express Feelings; Generate Great Potential If Acted**
**upon Mercury/Quincunx/ Uranus: Able to Tap into Higher Con-**
**sciousness, but Rejects Ideas as Implausible. Attracted to All New**
**Forms Of Communication. Aspect Creates Doubt In One's Self**

_____

_____

_____

_____

_____

_____

_____

_____

_____

_____

_____

_____

_____

_____

_____

BRIEF SUMMARY OF WORKSHEET:
MALE, JULY 3, 1919 (Father)

Even though the Sun is in the Sign of Cancer (more easy-going), Mercury is in the Sign of Leo. Therefore this man should never be embarrassed intellectually. Authoritative, and a born leader (president of trade organizations, leader in his field), his creative mind helped him to overcome his learning deficiencies. He is mentally ambitious. Mercury in a fixed sign would compel him to stay with something until he mastered it, and with Mercury in a fire sign, he would be his own harshest critic.

This is definitely someone who needs praise and reward for his efforts. Although his perception is slow, his mind is deliberate. It may take him longer to learn something, but he has a need to complete that task before going on to something new.

The most significant indicator in his chart is the planet Mercury sitting between Jupiter and Neptune. Jupiter expands his mind, he's interested in learning about everything (thirst for knowledge), and it allows him to retain a tremendous amount of information in his mind. Neptune, on the other hand, is the "Great Deceiver" enabling him to create an illusion and mask his learning deficiencies. It also would help him to deceive himself and perhaps negate any feelings of inadequacy within.

Mercury sextile the Moon enabled him to express his feelings and not suffer deep emotional concerns over his problem. Mercury quincunx Uranus (higher octave of Mercury) enabled him to tap into a higher consciousness for answers. In reading this chart we find he has very typical learning disability patterns. For example, excelling in sports and theatrical productions to over-compensate for any feelings of inferiority due to lack of comprehension. This would be a natural pattern because most people with dyslexia or similar learning disabilities have excellent coordination and superior memory skills. Excelling in other areas often makes teachers or parents feel the child is highly creative and therefore bored with the mundane tasks associated with basic learning skills, which is not always the case.

CASE HISTORY #5:
FEMALE, AUGUST 5, 1939

The subject was an extremely bright child who learned to talk very early. At two and a half years old she was reciting the entire alphabet, nursery rhymes, and singing songs such as "God Bless America," "The Marine Hymn," and "Anchors Aweigh" clearly and distinctly. By the time she went to kindergarten, she knew many of her favorite fairy tales, and "The Night Before Christmas" by heart. She had difficulty, however, learning to write her name.

Although her mother had obviously spent an enormous amount of time reading to her, when she tried to teach the little girl to write her name, the alphabet, or numbers the child grew restless and inattentive. She was very adept with her hands and loved to take things apart and put them back together again. Being ambidextrous, she used both hands equally well, favoring neither left or right.

Her problems in school started in the first grade. She had difficulty learning to read and write. She did not finish her work and always was pages behind the other children in her workbook. On her first report card she was labeled "lazy and inattentive". By the second grade she was frequently bringing unfinished work home to be signed. Her mother tried working with her and eventually she was able to grasp enough of the rudiments of reading, writing and simple arithmetic to allow her to pass into the third grade.

Throughout grammar school she was just a fair student and her report cards always labeled her as "lazy," "does not finish work on time" and "could do much better." Her teachers and parents were puzzled by the fact that she was an extremely bright child who could not seem to work up to her potential. Once she

97

did learn to read, however, she became an avid reader and developed a vast vocabulary. It should be noted that she can also read upside-down and backwards as easily as most people read conventionally. She was very creative, excelling in art and writing, and these talents carried over into her adult life.

Among her hobbies are creative writing, painting, sewing and crafts. She is often able to duplicate something just by looking at the way it is made. In high school, she had trouble with mathematics, failing both elementary algebra and geometry, but did well in science, art and language. Although she majored in art, the lack of passing math grades prevented her from attending college.

During our interview, the subject stated she has always had difficulty grasping abstract concepts and often feels she is missing some key element. This often leaves her feeling woefully ill-equipped for a specific task.

Instead of allowing her feelings of inadequacy to hinder her in any way, this woman made the most of her manual dexterity and creativity. For many years she earned her livelihood in the hairdressing field, as both a stylist and teacher. A number of years ago, she also undertook the management of her husband's small business, which forced her to learn bookkeeping and some accounting. Although she still has a problem with math and numbers, she says her husband has not gone bankrupt yet, so she must be doing something right!

As an amateur astrologer, she had to learn to cast charts by hand without the benefit of a computer, although she occasionally uses one to check her math. Like her father, her interests are varied and she continues on a quest for knowledge and self enlightenment despite her early dysfunction.

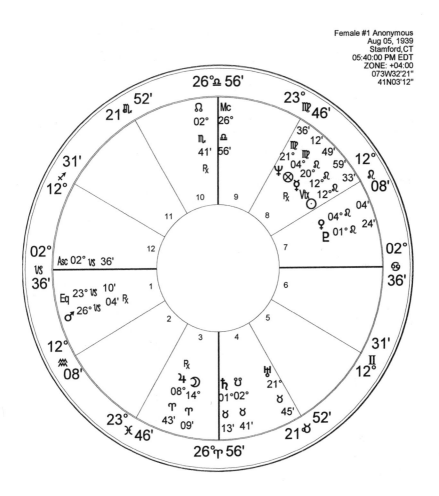

Female #1 Anonymous
Aug 05, 1939
Stamford, CT
05:40:00 PM EDT
ZONE: +04:00
073W32'21"
41N03'12"

AFA chart style

99

FEMALE #1
Saturday
Aug 5, 1939
5:40:00 PM
EDT   4:00
Stamford, CT
073W32'00"   41N03'00"

	Crd	Fix	Mut
Fir	2	4	0
Ear	2	2	1
Air	1	0	0
Wat	0	0	0

Symbol	Aspect Name	Exact
☌	Conjunction	000°00'
☍	Opposition	180°00'
△	Trine	120°00'
□	Square	090°00'
✶	Sextile	060°00'
∠	Semi-Square	045°00'
⋎	Semi-Sextile	030°00'
⊼	Quincunx	150°00'
⋔	Sesquiquadrate	135°00'

Moon in 3rd Quarter
Disseminating Type
Moon's Motion :
          + 12°05'23"
Moon is Slow
Sun/Moon Angle:
          241°36'

	☽	☉	☿	♀	♂	♃	♄	♅	♆	♇	☊	MC
☉	△											
☿	△	☌										
♀		☌										
♂				☍								
♃	☌	△	⋔	△								
♄			□	□								
♅		□	□		△	∠						
♆			⋎	∠	△		△					
♇			☌	☍	△	□	✶	✶				
☊		□		□	□		☍			□		
MC			✶	□	□		☍			□	☌	
Asc			⊼		□	△			⊼	✶	✶	

ANALYSIS WORKSHEET

The following worksheet is to be used merely to see how a person perceives and communicates. It is not to be used as a diagnostic tool for the detection of learning disabilities. It is an invaluable insight into the subject's interaction with others, communication skills, perception etc., even when no learning disability is present or suspected.

Fill in the blanks utilizing the information found in the book.

NAME: *Female*

BIRTH DATE: *August 5, 1939*

PLACE OF BIRTH: *Stamford, Connecticut*

TIME: *5:40 PM*

Astrological sign for Sun: *Leo*

Astrological sign for Mercury: *Leo*

Sun and Mercury in:

    (select one) **same sign**   different sign

Influence: *Strong Compatible Influence, Elaborate Vocabulary, Dramatic Thoughts and Words. Ability to Express Self. Understands and Communicates in Relation to Self.*

Mercury is in the Quality of:

    (select one) Cardinal **Fixed** Mutable

Influence: *Persistent, Sets Goals and Disregards Outside Influence, Expresses And Communicates Forcefully and Powerfully*

101

Mercury is in the Element of:
(select one) _Fire_ Earth Air Water

Influence: _**Enthusiastic, Energetic, Extremely Impatient in Communication. Relates Strongly Through Self**_

Mercury is in the __8th__ House. Intercepted? (yes _no_)

Influence: _**Deep, Penetrating Mind, Good Listener, Ability to Attain, Can Be Secretive or Caustic**_

The Moon is: (select one) Fast **Slow**

A: Perception is: _**Slow**_

B: Mercury is: (select one) ahead of, or **behind,** the Sun.

Influence: _**Deliberate Mind, Thinks Before Speaking**_

C: Combined influence of Sun, Moon and Mercury:

**Difficulty in Adapting to Change**

Mercury is Retrograde: (select one) **yes** no

**Influence: Causes Confusion, Inability to Make Decisions, Sometimes Misunderstood or Misquoted**

Mercury is: (select one) Casimi Combust

Influence:_____

Mercury is Conjunct the Planet _**Sun**_

Influence: _**Strong Ego, Relates Well to Self, Quick-Witted, Powerful Speaker and Thinker**_

List additional aspects to Mercury and their influences:

Mercury/Trine/Moon: Ability to Express Feelings With Great
Emotion, Good Conversationalist with a Sense of Humor Good
Listener, Expresses Compassion. Mercury/Square/Uranus: Ten-
dency to Appear Practical Even Though a Progressive Thinker,
Hard to Express Feelings of Being Different or Unique, Difficulty
in Expressing Intuitive Thoughts. Mercury/Sesquiquadrate/Jupi-
ter : Feelings of Frustration, Need to Persevere to Reach Goal.
Insecurity in Communicating Higher Level Subjects Such as Reli-
gion, Philosophy, Metaphysics. Mercury/Semi-Sextile/Neptune:
Lessons In Learning How to Express Psychic, Intuitive Thoughts
(ie., to be Comfortable Expressing "Gut Feelings")

_____

_____

_____

_____

_____

_____

_____

_____

_____

_____

_____

_____

_____

BRIEF SUMMARY OF WORKSHEET:
FEMALE, AUGUST 5, 1939

As you can see, this subject is a classic case of hereditary dyslexia. Inherited dyslexia seems to become less prominent in successive generations until the trait flares up again and displays an obvious pattern of dysfunction. This cycle of reoccurrence in families is what prompted the recent study which looked for, and found, a genetic factor linked to dyslexia.

Upon first meeting this subject, she appears to be very quiet and observant. When comfortable with the situation or her surroundings, she expresses herself with an elaborate vocabulary in a very animated and direct manner. If not fully understood when seeking information, she is not afraid to re-word her questions until she is satisfied with the answers she needs.

Since Mercury is the ruler of the sixth house in her chart, her daily existence is very linked to a questioning and understanding mode. Being dyslexic causes her to feel she doesn't always have the full picture, therefore she questions anything she does not fully understand. She is an advanced astrological student of mine, and it has become obvious to me that she has to relate every new concept I teach to herself in order to fully understand it. (Because her Mercury is in Leo - Fixed Fire). During class she will often say, "I think I understand, but I'll have to go home and work it out in my own way, on my own." "Her way" is probably a study pattern that she developed as a child. Because it works for her, it has become a habit that would be difficult to change.

She has compensated for her Retrograde Mercury by being very observant and has developed keen intuitive powers (Mercury in the Eight House). However, due to a lack of Air in her chart, she often feels she may not be getting her point across at the moment. So she will digress, giving elaborate explanations (Mercury in Jupiter), trying to give the listener a fuller picture of what she is telling them. This sometimes gives the impression of confusion, although she actually knows what she is trying to say. (You can see how in a classroom situation a teacher would sometimes view this as side-stepping the issue.) Often, in school if another student answered differently the same question she had been asked, she would say to herself "But that's what I just said."

In this chart Mercury only appears to be Conjunct the Sun and Venus, but since Pluto is Conjunct Venus (all in Leo), it creates a chain reaction. This combination makes for a good student, powerful speaker and natural diplomat. She is a person with good self-esteem and ego, while hiding the Pluto influence of a strong undercurrent that all is not below the surface. This gives the impression of a person who appears very self-confident, when in reality she must investigate and research whatever she doesn't understand in private. This is a face-saving device that often fools teachers.

With Mercury/Trine/Moon, you have a compassionate listener, who often states, "You need a good sounding board," to friends and colleagues. With this aspect the subject often masks her own emotions; while listening, she does not have to relate to her own problems.

Uranus being the higher octave of Mercury, with Mercury/Square/Uranus, she may appear practical but feel the need to seek new avenues of uniqueness. She has a need to think and feel differently, but often appears to conform.

CASE HISTORY #6:
FEMALE, JANUARY 3, 1952

The subject is a medical professional who attributes her early scholastic success to a photographic memory which she considers a gift. As a young child she was bright but when she started school she knew something was wrong and felt, as she puts it, that she just didn't fit in. Even though she couldn't learn to read in the first, second and third grades, she refused to believe she was stupid; in her mind she was just different.

Because she was having so much difficulty, her father took on the job of reading her school work to her and testing her verbally. It was always a source of disappointment to both of them when she came home with poor test scores after doing so well under her father's tutelage. Eventually she did learn to read. Aided by her photographic memory, a driving need to learn, and a very likeable personality she was able to make it through high school and get a college degree.

It was while in school for her medical specialty that she encountered a biology professor from her college days who was teaching one of her courses. He mentioned that he had just recently come across another student who had the same learning problem she had. Like her, he was highly intelligent but had to be tested verbally because he had a problem taking written tests. This was the first time anyone had recognized that she had a valid learning disability. Only then did she realize that those earlier problems she had to learn to compensate for had a name.

She says she still has one specific problem that she has had from childhood; the inability to understand and use phonics. This makes her unable to use a dictionary. If she looks up a word and it is broken up into syllables, it is impossible for her to read it or pronounce it. Once someone pronounces that word for her, she commits it to memory and never forgets it. She is able to pronounce it, read it and recognize it whenever she sees it.

She conducts and attends educational seminars in her field and is a strong motivational speaker who refuses to let a learning disability stand in her way.

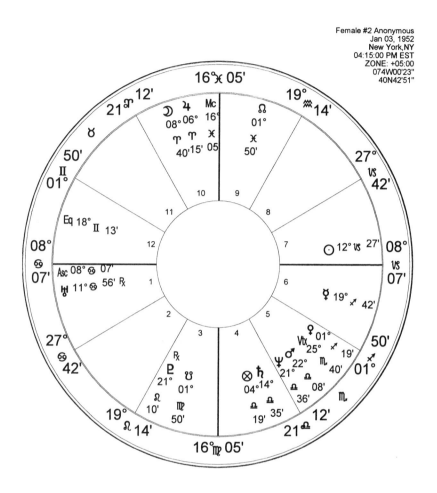

Female #2 Anonymous
Jan 03, 1952
New York,NY
04:15:00 PM EST
ZONE: +05:00
074W00'23"
40N42'51"

FEMALE #2
Thursday
Jan 3, 1952
4:15:00 PM
EST   + 5:00
New York, NY
073W57'00"   40N45'00"

	Crd	Fix	Mut
Fir	2	1	2
Ear	1	0	0
Air	3	0	0
Wat	2	0	1

	Aspect Name	Exact
☌	Conjunction	000°00'
☍	Opposition	180°00'
△	Trine	120°00'
□	Square	090°00'
✳	Sextile	060°00'
∠	Semi-Square	045°00'
⚺	Semi-Sextile	030°00'
⚻	Quincunx	150°00'
⚼	Sesquiquadrate	135°00'

Moon in 1st Quarter
Crescent Type
Moon's Motion :
    + 13°15'21"
Moon is Fast
Sun/Moon Angle:
    86°13'

	☽	☉	☿	♀	♂	♃	♄	♅	♆	♇	☊	MC
☉	□											
☿												
♀	△	∠										
♂		□	✳									
♃	☌	□			△							
♄	☍	□	✳	∠	☌	☍						
♅	□	☍			□	□						
♆		□	✳		☌		☌	□				
♇	⚼			△	✳	⚼	✳		✳			
☊				□	△		⚼					
MC		✳	□				⚻	△				
Asc	□	☍					□	□	☌	∠	△	△

ANALYSIS WORKSHEET

The following worksheet is to be used merely to see how a person perceives and communicates. It is not to be used as a diagnostic tool for the detection of learning disabilities. It is an invaluable insight into the subject's interaction with others, communication skills, perception etc., even when no learning disability is present or suspected.

Fill in the blanks utilizing the information found in the book.

NAME: *Female*

BIRTH Date: *January 3, 1952*

PLACE OF BIRTH: *New York City, New York*

TIME: *4:15 PM*

Astrological sign for Sun: *Capricorn*

Astrological sign for Mercury: *Sagittarius*

Sun and Mercury in:

    (select one)   same sign   **different sign**

Influence: *Expansive, Expressive Joviality of Sagittarian Speech by Mercury Masks The Serious Nature of the Capricorn Sun*

Mercury is in the Quality of:

    (select one)   Cardinal   Fixed   **Mutable**

Influence: *Harmonizing, Adaptable, Flexible*

Mercury is in the Element of:

(select one) **Fire** Earth Air Water

Influence: *Ardent, Purposeful, Impatient*

_____

_____

Mercury is in the __**6th**__ House.   Intercepted? (yes **no**)

Influence: *Good Managerial and Client Rapport, Detail-Minded,*
Efficient, Strong Work Ethics

_____

The Moon is: (select one)   **Fast** Slow

A: Perception is: *Quick Perception*

_____

_____

B: Mercury is: (select one) **ahead of**, or behind, the Sun.

Influence: *Eager Mind*

_____

_____

C: Combined influence of Sun, Moon and Mercury:

Tendency to Jump to Conclusions

_____

_____

Mercury is Retrograde: (select one) yes **no**

Influence:_____

_____

_____

_____

Mercury is: (select one)   Casimi   Combust
Influence:_____
_____

Mercury is Conjunct the Planet *None*_____
Influence:_____
_____

List additional aspects to Mercury and their influences:
Mercury/Sextile/Mars: a Harmonizing Relationship Between Mercury and Mars A Sharp Mind, Boundless Mental Energy. An Aggressive Thinker and Arguer. May Often Express Self Too Quickly Without Thinking. Mercury/Sextile/Saturn: Good Harmonizing Energy Between Planets. Mentally Ambitious and a Long Range Planner. Keeps Serious Issues Hidden. Authoritative Speaker. Ability to Overcome Inner Conflicts. Mercury/Sextile /Neptune: A Harmonizing Connection from the Conscious to the Subconscious. Often Works with Intuitive and Psychic Abilities. Vivid Imagination. Can Often Be a Role Player to Mask Any Shortcomings and Convince Herself That They Don't Exist. Can Be Extremely Inspirational. Mercury/Trine/Pluto: An Easy Flow Between Planets. Ability to Find out the "Whys and Wherefores" of Everything Very Easily. Able to Stay on Track of Goals for Change and Improvement. A Forward Looking, Resourceful Thinker with the Ability to Manipulate and Control Situations.

_____
_____
_____
_____

BRIEF SUMMARY OF WORKSHEET:
FEMALE, JANUARY 3, 1952

You will come across clients who complain of having had a difficult childhood due to a learning disability. They will then elaborate about problems that have spilled over into adulthood concerning perceiving and disseminating information. It is for this reason we have placed this particular chart and analysis in the book.

At first glance the subject appears to have very few classic indicators concerning conflicts to the planet Mercury. Yet, when reading the case history summary you can perceive all the difficulties this person has encountered. Therefore, you must remember the chart in itself may not always clearly indicate a learning disability. It is, however, a great diagnostic tool which indicates how one perceives, processes and expresses themselves. When a person has a problem with perception, processing and expressing, the chart gives an insight to the best way information should be presented so that it can be assimilated and communicated properly.

In our analysis of this subject's chart, one of the first things we discover is that she has an "out of sign" Mercury. Even though she is serious, organized and extremely work oriented (Capricorn Sun), she communicates on a carefree, jovial, optimistic level (Sagittarius Mercury). This was quite evident during our interview with her. Each time we touched on an area that was either too sensitive or personal, she covered up with witty remarks. Even though she appears to be well organized in her professional capacity, she was in a constant state of animation.

With Mercury ahead of the Sun, she often interrupted,

changed the subject and finished my sentences for me in a way that was charming and totally inoffensive. With Mercury in a Fire sign I found her to be receptive when I related to her on a personal level as long as I didn't over-step the bounds of privacy.

Mercury in a Mutable sign gives her the ability to do many things at one time. During our interview her phones rang, clients came into her office and yet she was able to handle it all without missing a beat, coming right back to the conversation, right on track. Some of this can be attributed to her fast Moon.

All her aspects to Mercury are positive and easy ones although, those same planets make hard or difficult aspects to her Sun--so she communicates, understands and expresses herself easily but the application is often difficult for her personally.

The aspect I find most significant in this chart is Mercury/Trine/Pluto. This gave her power and made her truly investigate every obstacle she encountered. With a slow and steady mind she is able to gather her resources and conquer any problem that threatens to stop her from change and improvement.

The best way for her to receive information is to have her relate to it on a personal level and to use various ways to pique her curiosity. She needs to have all the information before coming to a conclusion. She also needs to feel comfortable with anyone giving her the information.

Although she has a quick mind and is very confident, on observing her body language, she often places her hand over her mouth when speaking. This may be a trait left over from childhood when she was suffering from a lack of confidence due to her learning problems.

𝕿𝖍𝖊 𝕷𝖆𝖉𝖞'𝖘 𝕽𝖊𝖖𝖚𝖊𝖘𝖙

The Cast

Island	Man/Woman
Lord	Sun ☉
Lady	Moon ☽
Chancellor	Mercury ☿
Advisors	Planets
Treasury/Artistic	Venus ♀
Military/Workforce	Mars ♂
Spiritual/Law	Jupiter ♃
Responsibility/Commerce	Saturn ♄
Higher Thinking/Future Planner	Uranus ♅
Inspirational/Illusion Advisor	Neptune ♆
Inquisitor/Alchemist Advisor's	Pluto ♇

The Lady's Request:
An Allegory

Once upon a time there was a great kingdom known as Earth. Within this kingdom there existed a beautiful, independent island (man/woman). A strong and powerful Lord (☉) and his sensitive, beautiful Lady (☽) presided over this island. One day the Lady (☽) came to the Lord (☉) and said to him,

> "Do you know what I really would like? I want a new castle. I really need to have this castle because it would make me feel emotionally fulfilled and it would also be a wonderful dwelling for the entire staff."

The Lord (☉) thought about this request made by the Lady (☽). He always liked to please her. In some way she seemed to have much more insight and experience. He always prospered from her ideas and requests. When there was harmony between them, the island (man/woman) seemed to flourish.

The Lord (☉), however, was not a rash man and he decided to call upon his grand advisor and spokesperson, the Chancellor (☿). The Lord (☉) said to the Chancellor (☿),

> "The Lady (☽) wants to build a new castle. Please consult with all my under-advisors and let me know of the outcome before you announce the decision."

The Chancellor (☿) went first to the Treasury/Artistic Advisor (♀) and asked,

"Can we afford a new castle? Would it enhance this island (man/woman) to have this possession? Give me your answer quickly...!"

Next he visited the Military and Workforce Advisor (♂). The Chancellor (☿) told him (♂) about the Lady's (☽) request for a new castle. The Chancellor asked him (♂),

"Can we properly secure the new castle? Do we have enough workers to build it? Give me your answer quickly...!"

The Chancellor (☿) then consulted the Spiritual/Law Advisor (♃) telling him of the Lady's request. The Chancellor (☿) said,

"Check all the legal issues involved in building this new castle. As Spiritual Advisor (♃) you must base your answer on the moral consequences of the new castle. Give me your answer quickly...!"

The Chancellor (☿) then proceeded to the Office of Rules and Regulations where he could consult with the Responsibility/Commerce Advisor (♄). As he approached the old man (♄), the Chancellor (☿) could feel an aura of wisdom surrounding this esteemed advisor (♄). Once again, the Chancellor (☿) repeated the details of the Lady's (☽) request for a new castle. The Chancellor (☿) asked,

"Do you (♄) think that this castle would improve trade? Would we appear to be extraordinarily successful to the outside world? Would our image command respect? Also, don't we have the responsibility to fulfill the Lady's (☾) request? Give me your answer quickly...!"

Chancellor (☿) was now off to see the last three advisors. There were very special advisors. They were only called upon when important matters were to be considered. Therefore, they resided a little apart from the others.

The Chancellor (☿) had to cross over the rainbow bridge to connect with them and so he did. The first one he sought out was the Higher Thinking/Future Planner Advisor (♅). The Chancellor asked this advisor (♅),

> "Does the Lady's (☾) desire for a new castle fit in with the future plans for the island (man/woman)? Think this out beyond what seemed like a simple request. Give me your answer quickly...!"

The Chancellor (☿) went on to find the Inspirational/Illusion Advisor (♆). Once more he (♆) began to tell of the Lady's (☾) request. But, much to his (☿) surprise, the advisor (♆) already knew of the request for a new castle. The Chancellor (☿) asked,

> "Is this an inspirational idea that the Lady (☾) requested. Or, was she (☾) deluded into thinking the castle will fulfill her dreams? Give me your answer quickly...!

Last, but not least, the Chancellor (☿) visited the Inquisitor/Alchemist Advisor's (♇) laboratory. The Chancellor (☿) asked him (♇),

> "Can we make the transition from old to new smoothly, or is there any hidden motives in the Lady's request? Have you questioned her? Give me your answer quickly...!

After gathering the all answers the Chancellor (☿) returned to the Lord (☉) and quickly told the Lord (☉) the outcome. Now, with the power of the Lord (☉) behind him (☿), the Chancellor spoke the proclamation aloud....

What was the outcome? Was it for or against? Much of that would depend on the rapport (aspect) between the Chancellor (☿) and each Advisor (planet). If the rapport (aspect) was soft, agreement would flow easily. However, if the rapport (aspect) was hard, there would be misunderstandings and disagreements. Communication would not flow easily.

Remember, every thought, word and action goes through the process of combining the opinions (aspects) of all the planets before we act or react to anything. All of this takes just a "heart beat."

The Orton Dyslexia Society
National Office
8600 LaSalle Road
Chester Building, Suite 382
Baltimore, MD 21286-2044
(410) 296-0232
1-800-ABCD123

The Orton Dyslexia Society, founded in 1949 as a non-profit organization, was established to continue Dr. Samuel T. Orton's work in the study and treatment of dyslexia. The organization's membership includes concerned parents, educators, physicians, researchers, diagnosticians, speech and language therapists, and others in the field, as well as dyslexic individuals.

MERCURY EPHEMERIS

KEY:

♈	Aries	☉	Sun
♉	Taurus	☽	Moon
♊	Gemini	☿	Mercury
♋	Cancer	♀	Venus
♌	Leo	♂	Mars
♍	Virgo	♃	Jupiter
♎	Libra	♄	Saturn
♏	Scorpio	♅	Uranus
♐	Sagittarius	♆	Neptune
♑	Capricorn	♇	Pluto
♒	Aquarius		
♓	Pisces	℞	Retrograde

Jan 01, 1925 00:00 am EST

Date	☿ Geo Lon
01-01-1925	29° ♐ 28' ℞
01-08-1925	26° ♐ 52'
01-15-1925	00° ♑ 45'
01-22-1925	08° ♑ 00'
01-29-1925	16° ♑ 56'
02-05-1925	26° ♑ 50'
02-12-1925	07° ♒ 28'
02-19-1925	18° ♒ 48'
02-26-1925	00° ♓ 54'
03-05-1925	13° ♓ 48'
03-12-1925	27° ♓ 24'
03-19-1925	11° ♈ 00'
03-26-1925	22° ♈ 46'
04-02-1925	00° ♉ 26'
04-09-1925	02° ♉ 38' ℞
04-16-1925	29° ♈ 51' ℞
04-23-1925	25° ♈ 03' ℞
04-30-1925	22° ♈ 10' ℞
05-07-1925	23° ♈ 00'
05-14-1925	27° ♈ 22'
05-21-1925	04° ♉ 33'
05-28-1925	14° ♉ 01'
06-04-1925	25° ♉ 32'
06-11-1925	09° ♊ 00'
06-18-1925	23° ♊ 57'
06-25-1925	09° ♋ 11'
07-02-1925	23° ♋ 24'
07-09-1925	06° ♌ 03'
07-16-1925	17° ♌ 03'
07-23-1925	26° ♌ 19'
07-30-1925	03° ♍ 35'
08-06-1925	08° ♍ 15'
08-13-1925	09° ♍ 20' ℞
08-20-1925	06° ♍ 05' ℞
08-27-1925	00° ♍ 03' ℞
09-03-1925	26° ♌ 20' ℞
09-10-1925	29° ♌ 03'
09-17-1925	07° ♍ 52'
09-24-1925	19° ♍ 54'
10-01-1925	02° ♎ 38'

Oct 08, 1925 00:00 am EST

Date	☿ Geo Lon
10-08-1925	15° ♎ 01'
10-15-1925	26° ♎ 49'
10-22-1925	08° ♏ 03'
10-29-1925	18° ♏ 49'
11-05-1925	29° ♏ 10'
11-12-1925	09° ♐ 00'
11-19-1925	17° ♐ 58'
11-26-1925	24° ♐ 54'
12-03-1925	27° ♐ 03' ℞
12-10-1925	21° ♐ 08' ℞
12-17-1925	12° ♐ 38' ℞
12-24-1925	11° ♐ 24'
12-31-1925	16° ♐ 30'
01-07-1926	24° ♐ 35'
01-14-1926	04° ♑ 01'
01-21-1926	14° ♑ 11'
01-28-1926	24° ♑ 54'
02-04-1926	06° ♒ 10'
02-11-1926	18° ♒ 02'
02-18-1926	00° ♓ 34'
02-25-1926	13° ♓ 41'
03-04-1926	26° ♓ 41'
03-11-1926	07° ♈ 42'
03-18-1926	14° ♈ 00'
03-25-1926	13° ♈ 55' ℞
04-01-1926	08° ♈ 59' ℞
04-08-1926	04° ♈ 00' ℞
04-15-1926	02° ♈ 38'
04-22-1926	05° ♈ 21'
04-29-1926	11° ♈ 13'
05-06-1926	19° ♈ 28'
05-13-1926	29° ♈ 37'
05-20-1926	11° ♉ 30'
05-27-1926	25° ♉ 04'
06-03-1926	10° ♊ 01'
06-10-1926	25° ♊ 19'
06-17-1926	09° ♋ 37'
06-24-1926	22° ♋ 11'
07-01-1926	02° ♌ 51'
07-08-1926	11° ♌ 29'

Jul 15, 1926 00:00 am EST

Date	☿ Geo Lon
07-15-1926	17° ♌ 46'
07-22-1926	20° ♌ 59'
07-29-1926	20° ♌ 24' ℞
08-05-1926	16° ♌ 09' ℞
08-12-1926	11° ♌ 03' ℞
08-19-1926	09° ♌ 31'
08-26-1926	13° ♌ 54'
09-02-1926	23° ♌ 36'
09-09-1926	06° ♍ 16'
09-16-1926	19° ♍ 34'
09-23-1926	02° ♎ 23'
09-30-1926	14° ♎ 27'
10-07-1926	25° ♎ 47'
10-14-1926	06° ♏ 30'
10-21-1926	16° ♏ 36'
10-28-1926	25° ♏ 59'
11-04-1926	04° ♐ 13'
11-11-1926	10° ♐ 04'
11-18-1926	10° ♐ 52' ℞
11-25-1926	04° ♐ 01' ℞
12-02-1926	26° ♏ 10' ℞
12-09-1926	26° ♏ 17'
12-16-1926	02° ♐ 31'
12-23-1926	11° ♐ 22'
12-30-1926	21° ♐ 17'
01-06-1927	01° ♑ 42'
01-13-1927	12° ♑ 30'
01-20-1927	23° ♑ 40'
01-27-1927	05° ♒ 19'
02-03-1927	17° ♒ 28'
02-10-1927	00° ♓ 02'
02-17-1927	12° ♓ 23'
02-24-1927	22° ♓ 35'
03-03-1927	27° ♓ 25'
03-10-1927	25° ♓ 03' ℞
03-17-1927	18° ♓ 38' ℞
03-24-1927	14° ♓ 19' ℞
03-31-1927	14° ♓ 40'
04-07-1927	18° ♓ 57'
04-14-1927	25° ♓ 58'

Apr 21, 1927 00:00 am EST

Date	☿ Geo Lon
04-21-1927	04° ♈ 58'
04-28-1927	15° ♈ 34'
05-05-1927	27° ♈ 39'
05-12-1927	11° ♉ 13'
05-19-1927	26° ♉ 04'
05-26-1927	11° ♊ 20'
06-02-1927	25° ♊ 36'
06-09-1927	07° ♋ 57'
06-16-1927	18° ♋ 05'
06-23-1927	25° ♋ 49'
06-30-1927	00° ♌ 43'
07-07-1927	02° ♌ 12' ℞
07-14-1927	29° ♋ 59' ℞
07-21-1927	25° ♋ 28' ℞
07-28-1927	22° ♋ 03' ℞
08-04-1927	22° ♋ 51'
08-11-1927	28° ♋ 49'
08-18-1927	09° ♌ 19'
08-25-1927	22° ♌ 33'
09-01-1927	06° ♍ 23'
09-08-1927	19° ♍ 37'
09-15-1927	01° ♎ 57'
09-22-1927	13° ♎ 24'
09-29-1927	24° ♎ 03'
10-06-1927	03° ♏ 55'
10-13-1927	12° ♏ 49'
10-20-1927	20° ♏ 16'
10-27-1927	24° ♏ 58'
11-03-1927	24° ♏ 22' ℞
11-10-1927	16° ♏ 52' ℞
11-17-1927	09° ♏ 57' ℞
11-24-1927	11° ♏ 24'
12-01-1927	18° ♏ 41'
12-08-1927	28° ♏ 17'
12-15-1927	08° ♐ 39'
12-22-1927	19° ♐ 20'
12-29-1927	00° ♑ 13'
01-05-1928	11° ♑ 19'
01-12-1928	22° ♑ 43'
01-19-1928	04° ♒ 29'

Jan 26, 1928 00:00 am EST

☿

Date	Geo Lon
01-26-1928	16°♒30'
02-02-1928	28°♒07'
02-09-1928	07°♓24'
02-16-1928	10°♓45'℞
02-23-1928	06°♓18'℞
03-01-1928	29°♒10'℞
03-08-1928	26°♒04'℞
03-15-1928	28°♒03'
03-22-1928	03°♓35'
03-29-1928	11°♓27'
04-05-1928	20°♓58'
04-12-1928	01°♈50'
04-19-1928	14°♈01'
04-26-1928	27°♈30'
05-03-1928	12°♉10'
05-10-1928	27°♉16'
05-17-1928	11°♊23'
05-24-1928	23°♊21'
05-31-1928	02°♋42'
06-07-1928	09°♋09'
06-14-1928	12°♋16'
06-21-1928	11°♋45'℞
06-28-1928	08°♋19'℞
07-05-1928	04°♋30'℞
07-12-1928	03°♋21'
07-19-1928	06°♋26'
07-26-1928	13°♋50'
08-02-1928	25°♋03'
08-09-1928	08°♌45'
08-16-1928	23°♌04'
08-23-1928	06°♍42'
08-30-1928	19°♍17'
09-06-1928	00°♎50'
09-13-1928	11°♎25'
09-20-1928	21°♎01'
09-27-1928	29°♎24'
10-04-1928	06°♏00'
10-11-1928	09°♏27'
10-18-1928	07°♏27'℞
10-25-1928	29°♎37'℞

Nov 01, 1928 00:00 am EST

☿

Date	Geo Lon
11-01-1928	23°♎56'℞
11-08-1928	26°♎40'
11-15-1928	04°♏57'
11-22-1928	15°♏15'
11-29-1928	26°♏06'
12-06-1928	07°♐02'
12-13-1928	18°♐00'
12-20-1928	29°♐02'
12-27-1928	10°♑13'
01-03-1929	21°♑36'
01-10-1929	03°♒02'
01-17-1929	13°♒54'
01-24-1929	22°♒11'
01-31-1929	24°♒01'℞
02-07-1929	17°♒50'℞
02-14-1929	10°♒41'℞
02-21-1929	09°♒02'
02-28-1929	12°♒28'
03-07-1929	19°♒02'
03-14-1929	27°♒32'
03-21-1929	07°♓24'
03-28-1929	18°♓26'
04-04-1929	00°♈35'
04-11-1929	13°♈54'
04-18-1929	28°♈17'
04-25-1929	13°♉08'
05-02-1929	26°♉59'
05-09-1929	08°♊24'
05-16-1929	16°♊40'
05-23-1929	21°♊24'
05-30-1929	22°♊19'℞
06-06-1929	19°♊53'℞
06-13-1929	16°♊06'℞
06-20-1929	13°♊55'℞
06-27-1929	15°♊13'
07-04-1929	20°♊19'
07-11-1929	29°♊00'
07-18-1929	10°♋49'
07-25-1929	24°♋54'
08-01-1929	09°♌36'

Aug 08, 1929 00:00 am EST

Date	☿ Geo Lon
08-08-1929	23°♌36'
08-15-1929	06°♍26'
08-22-1929	18°♍04'
08-29-1929	28°♍32'
09-05-1929	07°♎49'
09-12-1929	15°♎37'
09-19-1929	21°♎16'
09-26-1929	23°♎21'Rx
10-03-1929	20°♎00'Rx
10-10-1929	12°♎16'Rx
10-17-1929	08°♎02'Rx
10-24-1929	12°♎02'
10-31-1929	21°♎15'
11-07-1929	02°♏15'
11-14-1929	13°♏34'
11-21-1929	24°♏46'
11-28-1929	05°♐50'
12-05-1929	16°♐49'
12-12-1929	27°♐48'
12-19-1929	08°♑47'
12-26-1929	19°♑39'
01-02-1930	29°♑42'
01-09-1930	06°♒56'
01-16-1930	07°♒18'Rx
01-23-1930	29°♑46'Rx
01-30-1930	23°♑07'Rx
02-06-1930	22°♑59'
02-13-1930	27°♑40'
02-20-1930	05°♒04'
02-27-1930	14°♒04'
03-06-1930	24°♒12'
03-13-1930	05°♓18'
03-20-1930	17°♓21'
03-27-1930	00°♈26'
04-03-1930	14°♈30'
04-10-1930	28°♈59'
04-17-1930	12°♉26'
04-24-1930	23°♉08'
05-01-1930	29°♉59'
05-08-1930	02°♊34'

May 15, 1930 00:00 am EST

Date	☿ Geo Lon
05-15-1930	01°♊06'Rx
05-22-1930	27°♉19'Rx
05-29-1930	24°♉15'Rx
06-05-1930	24°♉14'
06-12-1930	27°♉48'
06-19-1930	04°♊37'
06-26-1930	14°♊19'
07-03-1930	26°♊38'
07-10-1930	10°♋59'
07-17-1930	26°♋00'
07-24-1930	10°♌19'
07-31-1930	23°♌20'
08-07-1930	05°♍00'
08-14-1930	15°♍19'
08-21-1930	24°♍12'
08-28-1930	01°♎18'
09-04-1930	05°♎50'
09-11-1930	06°♎27'Rx
09-18-1930	01°♎56'Rx
09-25-1930	24°♍46'Rx
10-02-1930	22°♍14'
10-09-1930	27°♍27'
10-16-1930	07°♎32'
10-23-1930	19°♎12'
10-30-1930	01°♏00'
11-06-1930	12°♏30'
11-13-1930	23°♏41'
11-20-1930	04°♐38'
11-27-1930	15°♐25'
12-04-1930	26°♐02'
12-11-1930	06°♑18'
12-18-1930	15°♑31'
12-25-1930	21°♑36'
01-01-1931	20°♑33'Rx
01-08-1931	12°♑06'Rx
01-15-1931	06°♑19'Rx
01-22-1931	07°♑38'
01-29-1931	13°♑27'
02-05-1931	21°♑34'
02-12-1931	00°♒58'

Feb 19, 1931 00:00 am EST

Date	☿ Geo Lon
02-19-1931	11°≈17'
02-26-1931	22°≈24'
03-05-1931	04°✕19'
03-12-1931	17°✕08'
03-19-1931	00°♈47'
03-26-1931	14°♈49'
04-02-1931	27°♈47'
04-09-1931	07°♉36'
04-16-1931	12°♉45'
04-23-1931	12°♉52'℞
04-30-1931	09°♉14'℞
05-07-1931	05°♉06'℞
05-14-1931	03°♉36'
05-21-1931	05°♉45'
05-28-1931	11°♉12'
06-04-1931	19°♉20'
06-11-1931	29°♉50'
06-18-1931	12°♊31'
06-25-1931	27°♊02'
07-02-1931	12°♋16'
07-09-1931	26°♋49'
07-16-1931	09°♌58'
07-23-1931	21°♌35'
07-30-1931	01°♍39'
08-06-1931	10°♍01'
08-13-1931	16°♍14'
08-20-1931	19°♍29'
08-27-1931	18°♍33'℞
09-03-1931	13°♍13'℞
09-10-1931	07°♍11'℞
09-17-1931	06°♍30'
09-24-1931	12°♍54'
10-01-1931	23°♍47'
10-08-1931	06°♎07'
10-15-1931	18°♎23'
10-22-1931	00°♏12'
10-29-1931	11°♏31'
11-05-1931	22°♏26'
11-12-1931	03°♐02'
11-19-1931	13°♐16'

Nov 26, 1931 00:00 am EST

Date	☿ Geo Lon
11-26-1931	22°♐57'
12-03-1931	01°♑17'
12-10-1931	06°♑10'
12-17-1931	03°♑45'℞
12-24-1931	24°♐48'℞
12-31-1931	20°♐07'℞
01-07-1932	22°♐48'
01-14-1932	29°♐38'
01-21-1932	08°♑22'
01-28-1932	18°♑08'
02-04-1932	28°♑37'
02-11-1932	09°≈42'
02-18-1932	21°≈28'
02-25-1932	03°✕58'
03-03-1932	17°✕11'
03-10-1932	00°♈41'
03-17-1932	13°♈03'
03-24-1932	21°♈50'
03-31-1932	25°♈03'
04-07-1932	22°♈39'℞
04-14-1932	17°♈33'℞
04-21-1932	14°♈05'℞
04-28-1932	14°♈27'
05-05-1932	18°♈30'
05-12-1932	25°♈23'
05-19-1932	04°♉30'
05-26-1932	15°♉34'
06-02-1932	28°♉30'
06-09-1932	13°♊05'
06-16-1932	28°♊25'
06-23-1932	13°♋07'
06-30-1932	26°♋19'
07-07-1932	07°♌47'
07-14-1932	17°♌26'
07-21-1932	25°♌05'
07-28-1932	00°♍11'
08-04-1932	01°♍54'℞
08-11-1932	29°♌28'℞
08-18-1932	23°♌55'℞
08-25-1932	19°♌35'℞

Jun 08, 1933 00:00 am EST

Date	☿ Geo Lon
06-08-1933	29° ♊ 14'
06-15-1933	12° ♋ 22'
06-22-1933	23° ♋ 31'
06-29-1933	02° ♌ 33'
07-06-1933	09° ♌ 12'
07-13-1933	12° ♌ 51'
07-20-1933	12° ♌ 50' ℞
07-27-1933	09° ♌ 12' ℞
08-03-1933	04° ♌ 15' ℞
08-10-1933	02° ♌ 05'
08-17-1933	05° ♌ 16'
08-24-1933	13° ♌ 52'
08-31-1933	26° ♌ 07'
09-07-1933	09° ♍ 38'
09-14-1933	22° ♍ 52'
09-21-1933	05° ♎ 19'
09-28-1933	16° ♎ 58'
10-05-1933	27° ♎ 52'
10-12-1933	08° ♏ 06'
10-19-1933	17° ♏ 36'
10-26-1933	26° ♏ 00'
11-02-1933	02° ♐ 26'
11-09-1933	04° ♐ 43' ℞
11-16-1933	29° ♏ 51' ℞
11-23-1933	21° ♏ 05' ℞
11-30-1933	18° ♏ 56'
12-07-1933	24° ♏ 07'
12-14-1933	02° ♐ 43'
12-21-1933	12° ♐ 37'
12-28-1933	23° ♐ 02'
01-04-1934	03° ♑ 45'
01-11-1934	14° ♑ 47'
01-18-1934	26° ♑ 12'
01-25-1934	08° ♒ 02'
02-01-1934	20° ♒ 17'
02-08-1934	02° ♓ 33'
02-15-1934	13° ♓ 26'
02-22-1934	19° ♓ 53'
03-01-1934	18° ♓ 57' ℞
03-08-1934	12° ♓ 31' ℞

Sep 01, 1932 00:00 am EST

Date	☿ Geo Lon
09-01-1932	20° ♌ 50'
09-08-1932	28° ♌ 22'
09-15-1932	09° ♍ 59'
09-22-1932	22° ♍ 55'
09-29-1932	05° ♎ 41'
10-06-1932	17° ♎ 49'
10-13-1932	29° ♎ 17'
10-20-1932	10° ♏ 12'
10-27-1932	20° ♏ 37'
11-03-1932	00° ♐ 29'
11-10-1932	09° ♐ 33'
11-17-1932	16° ♐ 57'
11-24-1932	20° ♐ 34'
12-01-1932	16° ♐ 53' ℞
12-08-1932	07° ♐ 50' ℞
12-15-1932	04° ♐ 22'
12-22-1932	08° ♐ 21'
12-29-1932	16° ♐ 05'
01-05-1933	25° ♐ 25'
01-12-1933	05° ♑ 31'
01-19-1933	16° ♑ 07'
01-26-1933	27° ♑ 11'
02-02-1933	08° ♒ 46'
02-09-1933	20° ♒ 56'
02-16-1933	03° ♓ 41'
02-23-1933	16° ♓ 36'
03-02-1933	28° ♓ 15'
03-09-1933	05° ♈ 55'
03-16-1933	07° ♈ 03' ℞
03-23-1933	02° ♈ 23' ℞
03-30-1933	26° ♓ 45' ℞
04-06-1933	24° ♓ 38'
04-13-1933	26° ♓ 49'
04-20-1933	02° ♈ 21'
04-27-1933	10° ♈ 17'
05-04-1933	20° ♈ 05'
05-11-1933	01° ♉ 32'
05-18-1933	14° ♉ 36'
05-25-1933	29° ♉ 09'
06-01-1933	14° ♊ 29'

Mar 15, 1934 00:00 am EST

☿

Date	Geo Lon
03-15-1934	07°♓13'℞
03-22-1934	06°♓43'
03-29-1934	10°♓28'
04-05-1934	17°♓08'
04-12-1934	25°♓50'
04-19-1934	06°♈05'
04-26-1934	17°♈46'
05-03-1934	00°♉50'
05-10-1934	15°♉16'
05-17-1934	00°♊29'
05-24-1934	15°♊11'
05-31-1934	28°♊06'
06-07-1934	08°♋45'
06-14-1934	16°♋53'
06-21-1934	22°♋09'
06-28-1934	24°♋00'℞
07-05-1934	22°♋13'℞
07-12-1934	18°♋03'℞
07-19-1934	14°♋35'℞
07-26-1934	14°♋48'
08-02-1934	19°♋50'
08-09-1934	29°♋24'
08-16-1934	12°♌12'
08-23-1934	26°♌14'
08-30-1934	09°♍55'
09-06-1934	22°♍41'
09-13-1934	04°♎29'
09-20-1934	15°♎24'
09-27-1934	25°♎27'
10-04-1934	04°♏32'
10-11-1934	12°♏15'
10-18-1934	17°♏37'
10-25-1934	18°♏30'℞
11-01-1934	12°♏38'℞
11-08-1934	04°♏31'℞
11-15-1934	03°♏43'
11-22-1934	10°♏02'
11-29-1934	19°♏27'
12-06-1934	29°♏54'
12-13-1934	10°♐38'

Dec 20, 1934 00:00 am EST

☿

Date	Geo Lon
12-20-1934	21°♐30'
12-27-1934	02°♑30'
01-03-1935	13°♑44'
01-10-1935	25°♑14'
01-17-1935	06°♒59'
01-24-1935	18°♒35'
01-31-1935	28°♒35'
02-07-1935	03°♓46'
02-14-1935	00°♓54'℞
02-21-1935	23°♒20'℞
02-28-1935	18°♒59'℞
03-07-1935	20°♒06'
03-14-1935	25°♒09'
03-21-1935	02°♓41'
03-28-1935	11°♓54'
04-04-1935	22°♓27'
04-11-1935	04°♈13'
04-18-1935	17°♈14'
04-25-1935	01°♉27'
05-02-1935	16°♉26'
05-09-1935	00°♊58'
05-16-1935	13°♊33'
05-23-1935	23°♊27'
05-30-1935	00°♋18'
06-06-1935	03°♋45'
06-13-1935	03°♋31'℞
06-20-1935	00°♋19'℞
06-27-1935	26°♊35'℞
07-04-1935	25°♊16'
07-11-1935	27°♊52'
07-18-1935	04°♋33'
07-25-1935	14°♋58'
08-01-1935	28°♋14'
08-08-1935	12°♌43'
08-15-1935	26°♌49'
08-22-1935	09°♍53'
08-29-1935	21°♍50'
09-05-1935	02°♎43'
09-12-1935	12°♎33'
09-19-1935	21°♎11'

Sep 26, 1935 00:00 am EST

☿

Date	Geo Lon
09-26-1935	28°♎08'
10-03-1935	02°♏20'
10-10-1935	01°♏47'℞
10-17-1935	25°♎10'℞
10-24-1935	18°♎03'℞
10-31-1935	18°♎39'
11-07-1935	26°♎01'
11-14-1935	06°♏14'
11-21-1935	17°♏13'
11-28-1935	28°♏17'
12-05-1935	09°♐18'
12-12-1935	20°♐18'
12-19-1935	01°♑21'
12-26-1935	12°♑32'
01-02-1936	23°♑47'
01-09-1936	04°♒39'
01-16-1936	13°♒44'
01-23-1936	17°♒36'℞
01-30-1936	13°♒01'℞
02-06-1936	04°♒58'℞
02-13-1936	01°♒53'
02-20-1936	04°♒29'
02-27-1936	10°♒37'
03-05-1936	18°♒50'
03-12-1936	28°♒26'
03-19-1936	09°♓09'
03-26-1936	20°♓55'
04-02-1936	03°♈47'
04-09-1936	17°♈43'
04-16-1936	02°♉24'
04-23-1936	16°♉37'
04-30-1936	28°♉44'
05-07-1936	07°♊37'
05-14-1936	12°♊47'
05-21-1936	13°♊59'℞
05-28-1936	11°♊40'℞
06-04-1936	07°♊52'℞
06-11-1936	05°♊34'℞
06-18-1936	06°♊39'
06-25-1936	11°♊23'

Oct 02, 1936 00:00 am EST

☿

Date	Geo Lon
10-02-1936	06°♎18'℞
10-09-1936	01°♎26'℞
10-16-1936	04°♎34'
10-23-1936	13°♎31'
10-30-1936	24°♎39'
11-06-1936	06°♏10'
11-13-1936	17°♏33'
11-20-1936	28°♏42'
11-27-1936	09°♐41'
12-04-1936	20°♐35'
12-11-1936	01°♑26'
12-18-1936	12°♑07'
12-25-1936	22°♑06'
01-01-1937	29°♑39'
01-08-1937	01°♒02'℞
01-15-1937	24°♑01'℞
01-22-1937	16°♑39'℞
01-29-1937	15°♑57'
02-05-1937	20°♑27'
02-12-1937	27°♑49'
02-19-1937	06°♒46'
02-26-1937	16°♒48'
03-05-1937	27°♒44'
03-12-1937	09°♓35'
03-19-1937	22°♓22'
03-26-1937	06°♈06'
04-02-1937	20°♈24'
04-09-1937	04°♉01'
04-16-1937	15°♉01'
04-23-1937	22°♉01'
04-30-1937	24°♉26'
05-07-1937	22°♉38'℞
05-14-1937	18°♉36'℞
05-21-1937	15°♉38'℞
05-28-1937	15°♉52'
06-04-1937	19°♉40'
06-11-1937	26°♉34'
06-18-1937	06°♊09'
06-25-1937	18°♊13'
07-02-1937	02°♋21'

Jul 09, 1937 00:00 am EST

Date	☿ Geo Lon
07-09-1937	17°♋28'
07-16-1937	02°♌05'
07-23-1937	15°♌27'
07-30-1937	27°♌22'
08-06-1937	07°♍52'
08-13-1937	16°♍51'
08-20-1937	24°♍01'
08-27-1937	28°♍37'
09-03-1937	29°♍27' Rx
09-10-1937	25°♍24' Rx
09-17-1937	18°♍29' Rx
09-24-1937	15°♍22'
10-01-1937	19°♍49'
10-08-1937	29°♍39'
10-15-1937	11°♎29'
10-22-1937	23°♎31'
10-29-1937	05°♏14'
11-05-1937	16°♏32'
11-12-1937	27°♏32'
11-19-1937	08°♐16'
11-26-1937	18°♐46'
12-03-1937	28°♐54'
12-10-1937	08°♑04'
12-17-1937	14°♑31'
12-24-1937	14°♑31' Rx
12-31-1937	06°♑31' Rx
01-07-1938	29°♐52' Rx
01-14-1938	00°♑36'
01-21-1938	06°♑15'
01-28-1938	14°♑21'
02-04-1938	23°♑44'
02-11-1938	03°≈58'
02-18-1938	14°≈56'
02-25-1938	26°≈39'
03-04-1938	09°♓11'
03-11-1938	22°♓31'
03-18-1938	06°♈21'
03-25-1938	19°♈26'
04-01-1938	29°♈36'
04-08-1938	04°♉59'

Apr 15, 1938 00:00 am EST

Date	☿ Geo Lon
04-15-1938	04°♉57' Rx
04-22-1938	00°♉57' Rx
04-29-1938	26°♈38' Rx
05-06-1938	25°♈13'
05-13-1938	27°♈33'
05-20-1938	03°♉07'
05-27-1938	11°♉17'
06-03-1938	21°♉40'
06-10-1938	04°♊06'
06-17-1938	18°♊22'
06-24-1938	03°♋38'
07-01-1938	18°♋29'
07-08-1938	01°♌57'
07-15-1938	13°♌50'
07-22-1938	24°♌03'
07-29-1938	02°♍31'
08-05-1938	08°♍47'
08-12-1938	12°♍04'
08-19-1938	11°♍19' Rx
08-26-1938	06°♍22' Rx
09-02-1938	00°♍31' Rx
09-09-1938	29°♌22'
09-16-1938	05°♍06'
09-23-1938	15°♍45'
09-30-1938	28°♍14'
10-07-1938	10°♎48'
10-14-1938	22°♎51'
10-21-1938	04°♏20'
10-28-1938	15°♏20'
11-04-1938	25°♏55'
11-11-1938	06°♐05'
11-18-1938	15°♐40'
11-25-1938	24°♐00'
12-02-1938	29°♐17'
12-09-1938	27°♐55' Rx
12-16-1938	19°♐17' Rx
12-23-1938	13°♐36' Rx
12-30-1938	15°♐43'
01-06-1939	22°♐24'
01-13-1939	01°♑10'

Jan 20, 1939 00:00 am EST

Date	☿ Geo Lon
01-20-1939	10°♑57'
01-27-1939	21°♑22'
02-03-1939	02°♒20'
02-10-1939	13°♒54'
02-17-1939	26°♒08'
02-24-1939	09°♓03'
03-03-1939	22°♓20'
03-10-1939	04°♈48'
03-17-1939	14°♈02'
03-24-1939	17°♈35'
03-31-1939	15°♈04' ℞
04-07-1939	09°♈36' ℞
04-14-1939	05°♈57' ℞
04-21-1939	06°♈22'
04-28-1939	10°♈30'
05-05-1939	17°♈25'
05-12-1939	26°♈31'
05-19-1939	07°♉26'
05-26-1939	20°♉07'
06-02-1939	04°♊26'
06-09-1939	19°♊44'
06-16-1939	04°♋41'
06-23-1939	18°♋12'
06-30-1939	29°♋54'
07-07-1939	09°♌41'
07-14-1939	17°♌23'
07-21-1939	22°♌29'
07-28-1939	24°♌13' ℞
08-04-1939	21°♌55' ℞
08-11-1939	16°♌42' ℞
08-18-1939	12°♌31' ℞
08-25-1939	13°♌26'
09-01-1939	20°♌25'
09-08-1939	01°♍47'
09-15-1939	14°♍54'
09-22-1939	27°♍58'
09-29-1939	10°♎22'
10-06-1939	22°♎03'
10-13-1939	03°♏04'
10-20-1939	13°♏31'

Oct 28, 1939 00:00 am EST

Date	☿ Geo Lon
10-28-1939	24°♏42'
11-04-1939	03°♐32'
11-11-1939	10°♐39'
11-18-1939	13°♐57'
11-25-1939	10°♐06' ℞
12-02-1939	01°♐06' ℞
12-09-1939	27°♏48'
12-16-1939	02°♐04'
12-23-1939	10°♐04'
12-30-1939	19°♐36'
01-06-1940	29°♐49'
01-13-1940	10°♑27'
01-20-1940	21°♑29'
01-27-1940	02°♒58'
02-03-1940	14°♒59'
02-10-1940	27°♒30'
02-17-1940	10°♓10'
02-24-1940	21°♓36'
03-02-1940	29°♓01'
03-09-1940	29°♓36' ℞
03-16-1940	24°♓15' ℞
03-23-1940	18°♓32' ℞
03-30-1940	16°♓54'
04-06-1940	19°♓37'
04-13-1940	25°♓33'
04-20-1940	03°♈45'
04-27-1940	13°♈42'
05-04-1940	25°♈12'
05-11-1940	08°♉13'
05-18-1940	22°♉40'
05-25-1940	07°♊57'
06-01-1940	22°♊45'
06-08-1940	05°♋54'
06-15-1940	16°♋57'
06-22-1940	25°♋45'
06-29-1940	01°♌59'
07-06-1940	05°♌05'
07-13-1940	04°♌29' ℞
07-20-1940	00°♌36' ℞
07-27-1940	26°♋07' ℞

Aug 03, 1940 00:00 am EST

☿

Date	Geo Lon
08-03-1940	24°♋45'
08-10-1940	28°♋30'
08-17-1940	07°♌19'
08-24-1940	19°♌42'
08-31-1940	03°♍26'
09-07-1940	16°♍54'
09-14-1940	29°♍32'
09-21-1940	11°♎16'
09-28-1940	22°♎13'
10-05-1940	02°♏24'
10-12-1940	11°♏46'
10-19-1940	19°♏57'
10-26-1940	26°♏04'
11-02-1940	28°♏02'℞
11-09-1940	23°♏02'℞
11-16-1940	14°♏24'℞
11-23-1940	12°♏25'
11-30-1940	17°♏52'
12-07-1940	26°♏44'
12-14-1940	06°♐49'
12-21-1940	17°♐22'
12-28-1940	28°♐09'
01-04-1941	09°♑09'
01-11-1941	20°♑28'
01-18-1941	02°♒09'
01-25-1941	14°♒10'
02-01-1941	26°♒11'
02-08-1941	06°♓49'
02-15-1941	13°♓01'
02-22-1941	11°♓35'℞
03-01-1941	04°♓41'℞
03-08-1941	29°♒31'℞
03-15-1941	29°♒29'
03-22-1941	03°♓41'
03-29-1941	10°♓39'
04-05-1941	19°♓31'
04-12-1941	29°♓51'
04-19-1941	11°♈31'
04-26-1941	24°♈31'
05-03-1941	08°♉49'

May 10, 1941 00:00 am EST

☿

Date	Geo Lon
05-10-1941	23°♉56'
05-17-1941	08°♊37'
05-24-1941	21°♊31'
05-31-1941	02°♋00'
06-07-1941	09°♋46'
06-14-1941	14°♋27'
06-21-1941	15°♋36'℞
06-28-1941	13°♋17'℞
07-05-1941	09°♋11'℞
07-12-1941	06°♋26'℞
07-19-1941	07°♋30'
07-26-1941	13°♋04'
08-02-1941	22°♋50'
08-09-1941	05°♌44'
08-16-1941	19°♌57'
08-23-1941	03°♍52'
08-30-1941	16°♍49'
09-06-1941	28°♍43'
09-13-1941	09°♎40'
09-20-1941	19°♎40'
09-27-1941	28°♎37'
10-04-1941	06°♏06'
10-11-1941	11°♏08'
10-18-1941	11°♏40'℞
10-25-1941	05°♏43'℞
11-01-1941	27°♎49'℞
11-08-1941	27°♎12'
11-15-1941	03°♏46'
11-22-1941	13°♏28'
11-29-1941	24°♏07'
12-06-1941	04°♐59'
12-13-1941	15°♐54'
12-20-1941	26°♐54'
12-27-1941	08°♑03'
01-03-1942	19°♑24'
01-10-1942	00°♒56'
01-17-1942	12°♒15'
01-24-1942	22°♒00'
01-31-1942	26°♒57'
02-07-1942	23°♒40'℞

Feb 14, 1942 00:00 am EST

Date	☿ Geo Lon
02-14-1942	15°≈49' ℞
02-21-1942	11°≈43' ℞
02-28-1942	13°≈16'
03-07-1942	18°≈40'
03-14-1942	26°≈26'
03-21-1942	05°✶46'
03-28-1942	16°✶21'
04-04-1942	28°✶04'
04-11-1942	10°♈58'
04-18-1942	25°♈02'
04-25-1942	09°♉53'
05-02-1942	24°♉21'
05-09-1942	06°♊52'
05-16-1942	16°♊31'
05-23-1942	22°♊52'
05-30-1942	25°♊34'
06-06-1942	24°♊33' ℞
06-13-1942	21°♊02' ℞
06-20-1942	17°♊45' ℞
06-27-1942	17°♊16'
07-04-1942	20°♊39'
07-11-1942	27°♊48'
07-18-1942	08°♋24'
07-25-1942	21°♋45'
08-01-1942	06°♌21'
08-08-1942	20°♌40'
08-15-1942	03°♍55'
08-22-1942	15°♍58'
08-29-1942	26°♍53'
09-05-1942	06°♎40'
09-12-1942	15°♎09'
09-19-1942	21°♎51'
09-26-1942	25°♎40'
10-03-1942	24°♎45' ℞
10-10-1942	18°♎08' ℞
10-17-1942	11°♎20' ℞
10-24-1942	12°♎08'
10-31-1942	19°♎44'
11-07-1942	00°♏13'
11-14-1942	11°♏25'

Nov 21, 1942 00:00 am EST

Date	☿ Geo Lon
11-21-1942	22°♏38'
11-28-1942	03°♐43'
12-05-1942	14°♐43'
12-12-1942	25°♐43'
12-19-1942	06°♑45'
12-26-1942	17°♑47'
01-02-1943	28°♑23'
01-09-1943	07°≈11'
01-16-1943	10°≈50' ℞
01-23-1943	05°≈55' ℞
01-30-1943	27°♑44' ℞
02-06-1943	24°♑56'
02-13-1943	27°♑56'
02-20-1943	04°≈21'
02-27-1943	12°≈45'
03-06-1943	22°≈26'
03-13-1943	03°✶10'
03-20-1943	14°✶52'
03-27-1943	27°✶35'
04-03-1943	11°♈21'
04-10-1943	25°♈51'
04-17-1943	09°♉59'
04-24-1943	21°♉58'
05-01-1943	00°♊32'
05-08-1943	05°♊03'
05-15-1943	05°♊22' ℞
05-22-1943	02°♊23' ℞
05-29-1943	28°♉37' ℞
06-05-1943	27°♉01'
06-12-1943	28°♉55'
06-19-1943	04°♊18'
06-26-1943	12°♊46'
07-03-1943	24°♊04'
07-10-1943	07°♋43'
07-17-1943	22°♋39'
07-24-1943	07°♌17'
07-31-1943	20°♌47'
08-07-1943	02°♍57'
08-14-1943	13°♍47'
08-21-1943	23°♍17'

Aug 28, 1943 00:00 am EST

Date	☿ Geo Lon
08-28-1943	01°♎13'
09-04-1943	06°♎59'
09-11-1943	09°♎29'
09-18-1943	07°♎07'℞
09-25-1943	00°♎13'℞
10-02-1943	24°♍54'℞
10-09-1943	27°♍09'
10-16-1943	05°♎43'
10-23-1943	16°♎57'
10-30-1943	28°♎42'
11-06-1943	10°♏17'
11-13-1943	21°♏33'
11-20-1943	02°♐34'
11-27-1943	13°♐25'
12-04-1943	24°♐09'
12-11-1943	04°♑40'
12-18-1943	14°♑32'
12-25-1943	22°♑19'
01-01-1944	24°♑39'℞
01-08-1944	18°♑23'℞
01-15-1944	10°♑21'℞
01-22-1944	08°♑58'
01-29-1944	13°♑15'
02-05-1944	20°♑33'
02-12-1944	29°♑28'
02-19-1944	09°≈26'
02-26-1944	20°≈15'
03-04-1944	01°♓52'
03-11-1944	14°♓23'
03-18-1944	27°♓47'
03-25-1944	11°♈52'
04-01-1944	25°♈32'
04-08-1944	06°♉52'
04-15-1944	14°♉05'
04-22-1944	16°♉25'℞
04-29-1944	14°♉16'℞
05-06-1944	09°♉58'℞
05-13-1944	07°♉02'℞
05-20-1944	07°♉31'
05-27-1944	11°♉31'

Jun 03, 1944 00:00 am EST

Date	☿ Geo Lon
06-03-1944	18°♉30'
06-10-1944	28°♉00'
06-17-1944	09°♊49'
06-24-1944	23°♊43'
07-01-1944	08°♋50'
07-08-1944	23°♋44'
07-15-1944	07°♌26'
07-22-1944	19°♌37'
07-29-1944	00°♍19'
08-05-1944	09°♍25'
08-12-1944	16°♍38'
08-19-1944	21°♍18'
08-26-1944	22°♍18'℞
09-02-1944	18°♍38'℞
09-09-1944	12°♍02'℞
09-16-1944	08°♍31'℞
09-23-1944	12°♍12'
09-30-1944	21°♍41'
10-07-1944	03°♎38'
10-14-1944	15°♎56'
10-21-1944	27°♎53'
10-28-1944	09°♏21'
11-04-1944	20°♏24'
11-11-1944	01°♐08'
11-18-1944	11°♐33'
11-25-1944	21°♐34'
12-02-1944	00°♑40'
12-09-1944	07°♑23'
12-16-1944	08°♑22'℞
12-23-1944	01°♑03'℞
12-30-1944	23°♐33'℞
01-06-1945	23°♐35'
01-13-1945	29°♐03'
01-20-1945	07°♑07'
01-27-1945	16°♑30'
02-03-1945	26°♑41'
02-10-1945	07°≈33'
02-17-1945	19°≈04'
02-24-1945	01°♓19'
03-03-1945	14°♓21'

Mar 10, 1945 00:00 am EST

Date	☿ Geo Lon
03-10-1945	27°♓55'
03-17-1945	11°♈03'
03-24-1945	21°♈36'
03-31-1945	27°♈17'
04-07-1945	27°♈11'℞
04-14-1945	22°♈51'℞
04-21-1945	18°♈18'℞
04-28-1945	16°♈54'
05-05-1945	19°♈23'
05-12-1945	25°♈04'
05-19-1945	03°♉16'
05-26-1945	13°♉31'
06-02-1945	25°♉43'
06-09-1945	09°♊44'
06-16-1945	24°♊56'
06-23-1945	10°♋01'
06-30-1945	23°♋49'
07-07-1945	05°♌57'
07-14-1945	16°♌22'
07-21-1945	24°♌54'
07-28-1945	01°♍12'
08-04-1945	04°♍31'
08-11-1945	03°♍55'℞
08-18-1945	29°♌18'℞
08-25-1945	23°♌40'℞
09-01-1945	22°♌12'
09-08-1945	27°♌20'
09-15-1945	07°♍38'
09-22-1945	20°♍15'
09-29-1945	03°♎05'
10-06-1945	15°♎25'
10-13-1945	27°♎06'
10-20-1945	08°♏12'
10-27-1945	18°♏48'
11-03-1945	28°♏56'
11-10-1945	08°♐26'
11-17-1945	16°♐45'
11-24-1945	22°♐20'
12-01-1945	21°♐56'℞
12-08-1945	13°♐53'℞

Dec 15, 1945 00:00 am EST

Date	☿ Geo Lon
12-15-1945	07°♐13'℞
12-22-1945	08°♐38'
12-29-1945	15°♐10'
01-05-1946	23°♐57'
01-12-1946	03°♑45'
01-19-1946	14°♑08'
01-26-1946	25°♑01'
02-02-1946	06°♒25'
02-09-1946	18°♒24'
02-16-1946	01°♓01'
02-23-1946	14°♓03'
03-02-1946	26°♓32'
03-09-1946	06°♈12'
03-16-1946	10°♈12'
03-23-1946	07°♈40'℞
03-30-1946	01°♈51'℞
04-06-1946	27°♓59'℞
04-13-1946	28°♓22'
04-20-1946	02°♈33'
04-27-1946	09°♈31'
05-04-1946	18°♈33'
05-11-1946	29°♈21'
05-18-1946	11°♉47'
05-25-1946	25°♉49'
06-01-1946	11°♊00'
06-08-1946	26°♊08'
06-15-1946	09°♋57'
06-22-1946	21°♋54'
06-29-1946	01°♌50'
07-06-1946	09°♌35'
07-13-1946	14°♌39'
07-20-1946	16°♌21'℞
07-27-1946	14°♌10'℞
08-03-1946	09°♌14'℞
08-10-1946	05°♌17'℞
08-17-1946	06°♌00'
08-24-1946	12°♌30'
08-31-1946	23°♌33'
09-07-1946	06°♍46'
09-14-1946	20°♍08'

Sep 21, 1946 00:00 am EST

Date	☿ Geo Lon
09-21-1946	02°♎50'
09-28-1946	14°♎44'
10-05-1946	25°♎54'
10-12-1946	06°♏24'
10-19-1946	16°♏14'
10-26-1946	25°♏12'
11-02-1946	02°♐40'
11-09-1946	07°♐03'
11-16-1946	05°♐17'Rx
11-23-1946	26°♏49'Rx
11-30-1946	21°♏14'Rx
12-07-1946	23°♏57'
12-14-1946	01°♐29'
12-21-1946	10°♐56'
12-28-1946	21°♐09'
01-04-1947	01°♑44'
01-11-1947	12°♑39'
01-18-1947	23°♑55'
01-25-1947	05°♒38'
02-01-1947	17°♒49'
02-08-1947	00°♓15'
02-15-1947	12°♓02'
02-22-1947	20°♓44'
03-01-1947	22°♓58'Rx
03-08-1947	18°♓14'Rx
03-15-1947	11°♓47'Rx
03-22-1947	09°♓12'Rx
03-29-1947	11°♓18'
04-05-1947	16°♓50'
04-12-1947	24°♓43'
04-19-1947	04°♈21'
04-26-1947	15°♈28'
05-03-1947	28°♈00'
05-10-1947	11°♉58'
05-17-1947	27°♉02'
05-24-1947	12°♊07'
05-31-1947	25°♊50'
06-07-1947	07°♋26'
06-14-1947	16°♋40'
06-21-1947	23°♋16'

Jun 28, 1947 00:00 am EST

Date	☿ Geo Lon
06-28-1947	26°♋44'
07-05-1947	26°♋34'Rx
07-12-1947	23°♋08'Rx
07-19-1947	18°♋49'Rx
07-26-1947	17°♋04'
08-02-1947	19°♋57'
08-09-1947	27°♋44'
08-16-1947	09°♌26'
08-23-1947	23°♌11'
08-30-1947	07°♍03'
09-06-1947	20°♍07'
09-13-1947	02°♎15'
09-20-1947	13°♎28'
09-27-1947	23°♎52'
10-04-1947	03°♏23'
10-11-1947	11°♏46'
10-18-1947	18°♏20'
10-25-1947	21°♏26'
11-01-1947	18°♏21'Rx
11-08-1947	09°♏48'Rx
11-15-1947	05°♏29'
11-22-1947	09°♏27'
11-29-1947	17°♏56'
12-06-1947	28°♏02'
12-13-1947	08°♐38'
12-20-1947	19°♐26'
12-27-1947	00°♑23'
01-03-1948	11°♑32'
01-10-1948	22°♑58'
01-17-1948	04°♒42'
01-24-1948	16°♒33'
01-31-1948	27°♒32'
02-07-1948	05°♓11'
02-14-1948	05°♓41'Rx
02-21-1948	29°♒10'Rx
02-28-1948	22°♒52'Rx
03-06-1948	21°♒48'
03-13-1948	25°♒23'
03-20-1948	01°♓59'
03-27-1948	10°♓33'

Apr 03, 1949 00:00 am EST

Date	☿ Geo Lon
04-03-1949	02°♈52'
04-10-1949	16°♈37'
04-17-1949	01°♉15'
04-24-1949	15°♉46'
05-01-1949	28°♉34'
05-08-1949	08°♊25'
05-15-1949	14°♊44'
05-22-1949	17°♊11'
05-29-1949	15°♊53'Rx
06-05-1949	12°♊16'Rx
06-12-1949	09°♊11'Rx
06-19-1949	09°♊03'
06-26-1949	12°♊39'
07-03-1949	19°♊47'
07-10-1949	00°♋07'
07-17-1949	13°♋12'
07-24-1949	27°♋51'
07-31-1949	12°♌27'
08-07-1949	26°♌03'
08-14-1949	08°♍23'
08-21-1949	19°♍30'
08-28-1949	29°♍24'
09-04-1949	07°♎58'
09-11-1949	14°♎42'
09-18-1949	18°♎40'
09-25-1949	18°♎10'Rx
10-02-1949	12°♎09'Rx
10-09-1949	05°♎07'Rx
10-16-1949	04°♎57'
10-23-1949	12°♎04'
10-30-1949	22°♎34'
11-06-1949	03°♏58'
11-13-1949	15°♏22'
11-20-1949	26°♏34'
11-27-1949	07°♐36'
12-04-1949	18°♐32'
12-11-1949	29°♐26'
12-18-1949	10°♑17'
12-25-1949	20°♑45'
01-01-1950	29°♑40'

Jan 08, 1950 00:00 am EST

Date	☿ Geo Lon
01-08-1950	04°♒06'
01-15-1950	00°♒07'Rx
01-22-1950	21°♑34'Rx
01-29-1950	18°♑03'
02-05-1950	20°♑45'
02-12-1950	27°♑05'
02-19-1950	05°♒27'
02-26-1950	15°♒04'
03-05-1950	25°♒39'
03-12-1950	07°♓09'
03-19-1950	19°♓37'
03-26-1950	03°♈03'
04-02-1950	17°♈18'
04-09-1950	01°♉27'
04-16-1950	13°♉44'
04-23-1950	22°♉31'
04-30-1950	26°♉59'
05-07-1950	27°♉00'Rx
05-14-1950	23°♉42'Rx
05-21-1950	19°♉54'Rx
05-28-1950	18°♉32'
06-04-1950	20°♉42'
06-11-1950	26°♉14'
06-18-1950	04°♊41'
06-25-1950	15°♊45'
07-02-1950	29°♊09'
07-09-1950	14°♋02'
07-16-1950	28°♋57'
07-23-1950	12°♌48'
07-30-1950	25°♌15'
08-06-1950	06°♍18'
08-13-1950	15°♍55'
08-20-1950	23°♍55'
08-27-1950	29°♍46'
09-03-1950	02°♎23'
09-10-1950	00°♎24'Rx
09-17-1950	23°♍59'Rx
09-24-1950	18°♍23'Rx
10-01-1950	19°♍46'
10-08-1950	27°♍53'

Oct 15, 1950 00:00 am EST

Date	☿ Geo Lon
10-15-1950	09°♎10'
10-22-1950	21°♎09'
10-29-1950	02°♏57'
11-05-1950	14°♏22'
11-12-1950	25°♏27'
11-19-1950	06°♐17'
11-26-1950	16°♐55'
12-03-1950	27°♐18'
12-10-1950	07°♑03'
12-17-1950	15°♑00'
12-24-1950	18°♑09'Rx
12-31-1950	12°♑49'Rx
01-07-1951	04°♑15'Rx
01-14-1951	02°♑05'
01-21-1951	06°♑05'
01-28-1951	13°♑20'
02-04-1951	22°♑14'
02-11-1951	02°≈09'
02-18-1951	12°≈50'
02-25-1951	24°≈16'
03-04-1951	06°♓31'
03-11-1951	19°♓37'
03-18-1951	03°♈25'
03-25-1951	17°♈05'
04-01-1951	28°♈43'
04-08-1951	06°♉15'
04-15-1951	08°♉33'Rx
04-22-1951	06°♉04'Rx
04-29-1951	01°♉29'Rx
05-06-1951	28°♈33'Rx
05-13-1951	29°♈12'
05-20-1951	03°♉23'
05-27-1951	10°♉27'
06-03-1951	19°♉54'
06-10-1951	01°♊31'
06-17-1951	15°♊08'
06-24-1951	00°♋10'
07-01-1951	15°♋18'
07-08-1951	29°♋19'
07-15-1951	11°♌48'

Jul 22, 1951 00:00 am EST

Date	☿ Geo Lon
07-22-1951	22°♌41'
07-29-1951	01°♍55'
08-05-1951	09°♍12'
08-12-1951	13°♍55'
08-19-1951	15°♍02'Rx
08-26-1951	11°♍41'Rx
09-02-1951	05°♍26'Rx
09-09-1951	01°♍40'Rx
09-16-1951	04°♍39'
09-23-1951	13°♍42'
09-30-1951	25°♍42'
10-07-1951	08°♎16'
10-14-1951	20°♎28'
10-21-1951	02°♏07'
10-28-1951	13°♏17'
11-04-1951	24°♏01'
11-11-1951	04°♐24'
11-18-1951	14°♐19'
11-25-1951	23°♐21'
12-02-1951	00°♑15'
12-09-1951	02°♑04'Rx
12-16-1951	25°♐38'Rx
12-23-1951	17°♐26'Rx
12-30-1951	16°♐39'
01-06-1952	21°♐51'
01-13-1952	29°♐54'
01-20-1952	09°♑18'
01-27-1952	19°♑28'
02-03-1952	00°≈13'
02-10-1952	11°≈34'
02-17-1952	23°≈35'
02-24-1952	06°♓18'
03-02-1952	19°♓36'
03-09-1952	02°♈42'
03-16-1952	13°♈35'
03-23-1952	19°♈41'
03-30-1952	19°♈38'Rx
04-06-1952	14°♈59'Rx
04-13-1952	10°♈09'Rx
04-20-1952	08°♈44'

Apr 27, 1952 00:00 am EST	
	☿
Date	Geo Lon
04-27-1952	11°♈19'
05-04-1952	17°♈06'
05-11-1952	25°♈17'
05-18-1952	05°♉27'
05-25-1952	17°♉26'
06-01-1952	01°♊10'
06-08-1952	16°♊14'
06-15-1952	01°♋29'
06-22-1952	15°♋36'
06-29-1952	28°♋01'
07-06-1952	08°♌36'
07-13-1952	17°♌13'
07-20-1952	23°♌33'
07-27-1952	26°♌52'
08-03-1952	26°♌21'℞
08-10-1952	22°♌00'℞
08-17-1952	16°♌39'℞
08-24-1952	15°♌02'
08-31-1952	19°♌36'
09-07-1952	29°♌30'
09-14-1952	12°♍09'
09-21-1952	25°♍17'
09-28-1952	07°♎54'
10-05-1952	19°♎48'
10-12-1952	01°♏02'
10-19-1952	11°♏42'
10-26-1952	21°♏50'
11-02-1952	01°♐16'
11-09-1952	09°♐32'
11-16-1952	15°♐21'
11-23-1952	15°♐48'℞
11-30-1952	08°♐30'℞
12-07-1952	01°♐00'℞
12-14-1952	01°♐35'
12-21-1952	07°♐54'
12-28-1952	16°♐43'
01-04-1953	26°♐34'
01-11-1953	06°♑57'
01-18-1953	17°♑46'
01-25-1953	29°♑02'

Feb 01, 1953 00:00 am EST	
	☿
Date	Geo Lon
02-01-1953	10°♒48'
02-08-1953	23°♒07'
02-15-1953	05°♓53'
02-22-1953	18°♓19'
03-01-1953	28°♓22'
03-08-1953	02°♈56'
03-15-1953	00°♈32'℞
03-22-1953	24°♓22'℞
03-29-1953	20°♓12'℞
04-05-1953	20°♓31'
04-12-1953	24°♓43'
04-19-1953	01°♈42'
04-26-1953	10°♈41'
05-03-1953	21°♈20'
05-10-1953	03°♉33'
05-17-1953	17°♉17'
05-24-1953	02°♊17'
05-31-1953	17°♊32'
06-07-1953	01°♋38'
06-14-1953	13°♋51'
06-21-1953	23°♋56'
06-28-1953	01°♌42'
07-05-1953	06°♌44'
07-12-1953	08°♌22'℞
07-19-1953	06°♌14'℞
07-26-1953	01°♌34'℞
08-02-1953	27°♋52'℞
08-09-1953	28°♋32'
08-16-1953	04°♌37'
08-23-1953	15°♌18'
08-30-1953	28°♌32'
09-06-1953	12°♍11'
09-13-1953	25°♍13'
09-20-1953	07°♎22'
09-27-1953	18°♎42'
10-04-1953	29°♎17'
10-11-1953	09°♏09'
10-18-1953	18°♏05'
10-25-1953	25°♏34'
11-01-1953	00°♐12'

Nov 08, 1953 00:00 am EST

Date	☿ Geo Lon
11-08-1953	29°♏16'℞
11-15-1953	21°♏24'℞
11-22-1953	14°♏52'℞
11-29-1953	16°♏47'
12-06-1953	24°♏08'
12-13-1953	03°♐39'
12-20-1953	13°♐57'
12-27-1953	24°♐35'
01-03-1954	05°♑27'
01-10-1954	16°♑37'
01-17-1954	28°♑08'
01-24-1954	10°♒03'
01-31-1954	22°♒15'
02-07-1954	03°♓58'
02-14-1954	13°♓05'
02-21-1954	16°♓04'℞
02-28-1954	11°♓31'℞
03-07-1954	04°♓39'℞
03-14-1954	01°♓43'℞
03-21-1954	03°♓41'
03-28-1954	09°♓12'
04-04-1954	17°♓03'
04-11-1954	26°♓35'
04-18-1954	07°♈33'
04-25-1954	19°♈51'
05-02-1954	03°♉30'
05-09-1954	18°♉20'
05-16-1954	03°♊28'
05-23-1954	17°♊27'
05-30-1954	29°♊18'
06-06-1954	08°♋38'
06-13-1954	15°♋12'
06-20-1954	18°♋31'
06-27-1954	18°♋12'℞
07-04-1954	14°♋49'℞
07-11-1954	10°♋47'℞
07-18-1954	09°♋19'
07-25-1954	12°♋14'
08-01-1954	19°♋42'
08-08-1954	01°♌05'

Aug 15, 1954 00:00 am EST

Date	☿ Geo Lon
08-15-1954	14°♌49'
08-22-1954	28°♌57'
08-29-1954	12°♍22'
09-05-1954	24°♍47'
09-12-1954	06°♎12'
09-19-1954	16°♎42'
09-26-1954	26°♎17'
10-03-1954	04°♏41'
10-10-1954	11°♏18'
10-17-1954	14°♏41'
10-24-1954	12°♏21'℞
10-31-1954	04°♏15'℞
11-07-1954	28°♎57'℞
11-14-1954	02°♏08'
11-21-1954	10°♏28'
11-28-1954	20°♏41'
12-05-1954	01°♐25'
12-12-1954	12°♐17'
12-19-1954	23°♐13'
12-26-1954	04°♑18'
01-02-1955	15°♑34'
01-09-1955	27°♑05'
01-16-1955	08°♒41'
01-23-1955	19°♒39'
01-30-1955	27°♒46'
02-06-1955	29°♒09'℞
02-13-1955	22°♒50'℞
02-20-1955	15°♒59'℞
02-27-1955	14°♒32'
03-06-1955	17°♒58'
03-13-1955	24°♒31'
03-20-1955	03°♓01'
03-27-1955	12°♓56'
04-03-1955	24°♓04'
04-10-1955	06°♈21'
04-17-1955	19°♈51'
04-24-1955	04°♉26'
05-01-1955	19°♉20'
05-08-1955	03°♊05'
05-15-1955	14°♊22'

May 22, 1955 00:00 am EST

Date	☿ Geo Lon
05-22-1955	22° ♊ 39'
05-29-1955	27° ♊ 34'
06-05-1955	28° ♊ 47' ℞
06-12-1955	26° ♊ 34' ℞
06-19-1955	22° ♊ 44' ℞
06-26-1955	20° ♊ 16' ℞
07-03-1955	21° ♊ 16'
07-10-1955	26° ♊ 13'
07-17-1955	04° ♋ 55'
07-24-1955	16° ♋ 53'
07-31-1955	01° ♌ 01'
08-07-1955	15° ♌ 35'
08-14-1955	29° ♌ 22'
08-21-1955	12° ♍ 00'
08-28-1955	23° ♍ 29'
09-04-1955	03° ♎ 53'
09-11-1955	13° ♎ 08'
09-18-1955	20° ♎ 56'
09-25-1955	26° ♎ 36'
10-02-1955	28° ♎ 37' ℞
10-09-1955	24° ♎ 59' ℞
10-16-1955	17° ♎ 02' ℞
10-23-1955	13° ♎ 11'
10-30-1955	17° ♎ 35'
11-06-1955	26° ♎ 51'
11-13-1955	07° ♏ 44'
11-20-1955	18° ♏ 55'
11-27-1955	00° ♐ 02'
12-04-1955	11° ♐ 03'
12-11-1955	22° ♐ 03'
12-18-1955	03° ♑ 05'
12-25-1955	14° ♑ 12'
01-01-1956	25° ♑ 12'
01-08-1956	05° ♒ 20'
01-15-1956	12° ♒ 23'
01-22-1956	12° ♒ 14' ℞
01-29-1956	04° ♒ 34' ℞
02-05-1956	28° ♑ 18' ℞
02-12-1956	28° ♑ 22'
02-19-1956	03° ♒ 05'

Feb 26, 1956 00:00 am EST

Date	☿ Geo Lon
02-26-1956	10° ♒ 28'
03-04-1956	19° ♒ 28'
03-11-1956	29° ♒ 39'
03-18-1956	10° ♓ 51'
03-25-1956	23° ♓ 03'
04-01-1956	06° ♈ 19'
04-08-1956	20° ♈ 34'
04-15-1956	05° ♉ 09'
04-22-1956	18° ♉ 32'
04-29-1956	29° ♉ 06'
05-06-1956	05° ♊ 59'
05-13-1956	08° ♊ 48'
05-20-1956	07° ♊ 40' ℞
05-27-1956	04° ♊ 02' ℞
06-03-1956	00° ♊ 51' ℞
06-10-1956	00° ♊ 32'
06-17-1956	03° ♊ 51'
06-24-1956	10° ♊ 32'
07-01-1956	20° ♊ 15'
07-08-1956	02° ♋ 43'
07-15-1956	17° ♋ 08'
07-22-1956	02° ♌ 03'
07-29-1956	16° ♌ 09'
08-05-1956	28° ♌ 59'
08-12-1956	10° ♍ 30'
08-19-1956	20° ♍ 45'
08-26-1956	29° ♍ 36'
09-02-1956	06° ♎ 42'
09-09-1956	11° ♎ 15'
09-16-1956	11° ♎ 49' ℞
09-23-1956	07° ♎ 03' ℞
09-30-1956	29° ♍ 43' ℞
10-07-1956	27° ♍ 30'
10-14-1956	03° ♎ 06'
10-21-1956	13° ♎ 13'
10-28-1956	24° ♎ 46'
11-04-1956	06° ♏ 24'
11-11-1956	17° ♏ 47'
11-18-1956	28° ♏ 54'
11-25-1956	09° ♐ 50'

Dec 02, 1956 00:00 am EST

Date	☿ Geo Lon
12-02-1956	20°♐40'
12-09-1956	01°♑23'
12-16-1956	11°♑46'
12-23-1956	21°♑03'
12-30-1956	26°♑56'
01-06-1957	25°♑20'℞
01-13-1957	16°♑47'℞
01-20-1957	11°♑27'℞
01-27-1957	12°♑58'
02-03-1957	18°♑49'
02-10-1957	26°♑54'
02-17-1957	06°♒19'
02-24-1957	16°♒40'
03-03-1957	27°♒52'
03-10-1957	09°♓56'
03-17-1957	22°♓56'
03-24-1957	06°♈47'
03-31-1957	20°♈56'
04-07-1957	03°♉50'
04-14-1957	13°♉30'
04-21-1957	18°♉40'
04-28-1957	19°♉03'℞
05-05-1957	15°♉44'℞
05-12-1957	11°♉40'℞
05-19-1957	09°♉59'
05-26-1957	11°♉55'
06-02-1957	17°♉10'
06-09-1957	25°♉14'
06-16-1957	05°♊46'
06-23-1957	18°♊36'
06-30-1957	03°♋13'
07-07-1957	18°♋23'
07-14-1957	02°♌45'
07-21-1957	15°♌42'
07-28-1957	27°♌11'
08-04-1957	07°♍11'
08-11-1957	15°♍31'
08-18-1957	21°♍46'
08-25-1957	25°♍02'
09-01-1957	24°♍04'℞

Sep 08, 1957 00:00 am EST

Date	☿ Geo Lon
09-08-1957	18°♍32'℞
09-15-1957	12°♍21'℞
09-22-1957	11°♍54'
09-29-1957	18°♍38'
10-06-1957	29°♍34'
10-13-1957	11°♎45'
10-20-1957	23°♎50'
10-27-1957	05°♏31'
11-03-1957	16°♏45'
11-10-1957	27°♏38'
11-17-1957	08°♐15'
11-24-1957	18°♐34'
12-01-1957	28°♐21'
12-08-1957	06°♑43'
12-15-1957	11°♑24'
12-22-1957	08°♑25'℞
12-29-1957	29°♐26'℞
01-05-1958	25°♐14'℞
01-12-1958	28°♐08'
01-19-1958	04°♑58'
01-26-1958	13°♑41'
02-02-1958	23°♑26'
02-09-1958	03°♒56'
02-16-1958	15°♒06'
02-23-1958	27°♒00'
03-02-1958	09°♓41'
03-09-1958	23°♓06'
03-16-1958	06°♈44'
03-23-1958	19°♈02'
03-30-1958	27°♈38'
04-06-1958	00°♉50'
04-13-1958	28°♈40'℞
04-20-1958	23°♈49'℞
04-27-1958	20°♈23'℞
05-04-1958	20°♈36'
05-11-1958	24°♈29'
05-18-1958	01°♉16'
05-25-1958	10°♉22'
06-01-1958	21°♉30'
06-08-1958	04°♊34'

Jun 15, 1958 00:00 am EST

Date	☿ Geo Lon
06-15-1958	19°Ⅱ17'
06-22-1958	04°♋36'
06-29-1958	19°♋08'
07-06-1958	02°♌09'
07-13-1958	13°♌29'
07-20-1958	23°♌06'
07-27-1958	00°♍45'
08-03-1958	05°♍55'
08-10-1958	07°♍41'℞
08-17-1958	05°♍13'℞
08-24-1958	29°♌28'℞
08-31-1958	24°♌59'℞
09-07-1958	26°♌23'
09-14-1958	04°♍11'
09-21-1958	15°♍51'
09-28-1958	28°♍39'
10-05-1958	11°♎13'
10-12-1958	23°♎10'
10-19-1958	04°♏33'
10-26-1958	15°♏24'
11-02-1958	25°♏49'
11-09-1958	05°♐45'
11-16-1958	14°♐53'
11-23-1958	22°♐18'
11-30-1958	25°♐42'
12-07-1958	21°♐27'℞
12-14-1958	12°♐27'℞
12-21-1958	09°♐31'
12-28-1958	13°♐42'
01-04-1959	21°♐25'
01-11-1959	00°♑42'
01-18-1959	10°♑47'
01-25-1959	21°♑23'
02-01-1959	02°♒31'
02-08-1959	14°♒13'
02-15-1959	26°♒34'
02-22-1959	09°♓30'
03-01-1959	22°♓34'
03-08-1959	04°♈10'
03-15-1959	11°♈35'

Mar 22, 1959 00:00 am EST

Date	☿ Geo Lon
03-22-1959	12°♈38'℞
03-29-1959	08°♈10'℞
04-05-1959	02°♈44'℞
04-12-1959	00°♈38'
04-19-1959	02°♈44'
04-26-1959	08°♈10'
05-03-1959	16°♈04'
05-10-1959	25°♈53'
05-17-1959	07°♉25'
05-24-1959	20°♉38'
05-31-1959	05°Ⅱ20'
06-07-1959	20°Ⅱ41'
06-14-1959	05°♋18'
06-21-1959	18°♋16'
06-28-1959	29°♋19'
07-05-1959	08°♌20'
07-12-1959	15°♌03'
07-19-1959	18°♌49'
07-26-1959	18°♌55'℞
08-02-1959	15°♌13'℞
08-09-1959	10°♌03'℞
08-16-1959	07°♌41'
08-23-1959	10°♌57'
08-30-1959	19°♌45'
09-06-1959	02°♍04'
09-13-1959	15°♍27'
09-20-1959	28°♍28'
09-27-1959	10°♎44'
10-04-1959	22°♎15'
10-11-1959	03°♏06'
10-18-1959	13°♏19'
10-25-1959	22°♏50'
11-01-1959	01°♐18'
11-08-1959	07°♐43'
11-15-1959	09°♐47'℞
11-22-1959	04°♐25'℞
11-29-1959	25°♏45'℞
12-06-1959	24°♏09'
12-13-1959	29°♏31'
12-20-1959	08°♐05'

Dec 27, 1959 00:00 am EST

Date	☿ Geo Lon
12-27-1959	17°♐54'
01-03-1960	28°♐16'
01-10-1960	09°♑00'
01-17-1960	20°♑05'
01-24-1960	01°♒35'
01-31-1960	13°♒35'
02-07-1960	26°♒01'
02-14-1960	08°♓26'
02-21-1960	19°♓15'
02-28-1960	25°♓24'
03-06-1960	24°♓18'℞
03-13-1960	18°♓03'℞
03-20-1960	12°♓57'℞
03-27-1960	12°♓29'
04-03-1960	16°♓11'
04-10-1960	22°♓49'
04-17-1960	01°♈30'
04-24-1960	11°♈48'
05-01-1960	23°♈35'
05-08-1960	06°♉49'
05-15-1960	21°♉25'
05-22-1960	06°♊41'
05-29-1960	21°♊17'
06-05-1960	04°♋04'
06-12-1960	14°♋38'
06-19-1960	22°♋47'
06-26-1960	28°♋11'
07-03-1960	00°♌14'
07-10-1960	28°♋35'℞
07-17-1960	24°♋18'℞
07-24-1960	20°♋33'℞
07-31-1960	20°♋34'
08-07-1960	25°♋36'
08-14-1960	05°♌20'
08-21-1960	18°♌13'
08-28-1960	02°♍08'
09-04-1960	15°♍36'
09-11-1960	28°♍10'
09-18-1960	09°♎50'
09-25-1960	20°♎39'

Oct 02, 1960 00:00 am EST

Date	☿ Geo Lon
10-02-1960	00°♏40'
10-09-1960	09°♏46'
10-16-1960	17°♏31'
10-23-1960	22°♏52'
10-30-1960	23°♏32'℞
11-06-1960	17°♏14'℞
11-13-1960	09°♏15'℞
11-20-1960	09°♏00'
11-27-1960	15°♏30'
12-04-1960	24°♏52'
12-11-1960	05°♐12'
12-18-1960	15°♐52'
12-25-1960	26°♐43'
01-01-1961	07°♑45'
01-08-1961	19°♑04'
01-15-1961	00°♒42'
01-22-1961	12°♒38'
01-29-1961	24°♒21'
02-05-1961	04°♓18'
02-12-1961	09°♓07'
02-19-1961	06°♓00'℞
02-26-1961	28°♒38'℞
03-05-1961	24°♒30'℞
03-12-1961	25°♒40'
03-19-1961	00°♓42'
03-26-1961	08°♓14'
04-02-1961	17°♓28'
04-09-1961	28°♓05'
04-16-1961	09°♈58'
04-23-1961	23°♈09'
04-30-1961	07°♉33'
05-07-1961	22°♉38'
05-14-1961	07°♊05'
05-21-1961	19°♊32'
05-28-1961	29°♊23'
06-04-1961	06°♋20'
06-11-1961	09°♋59'
06-18-1961	10°♋00'℞
06-25-1961	06°♋55'℞
07-02-1961	03°♋00'℞

Jul 09, 1961 00:00 am EST

Date	☿ Geo Lon
07-09-1961	01°♋21'
07-16-1961	03°♋44'
07-23-1961	10°♋24'
07-30-1961	20°♋57'
08-06-1961	04°♌19'
08-13-1961	18°♌41'
08-20-1961	02°♍35'
08-27-1961	15°♍27'
09-03-1961	27°♍14'
09-10-1961	08°♎02'
09-17-1961	17°♎49'
09-24-1961	26°♎27'
10-01-1961	03°♏26'
10-08-1961	07°♏36'
10-15-1961	06°♏50'Rx
10-22-1961	29°♎52'Rx
10-29-1961	22°♎56'Rx
11-05-1961	24°♎02'
11-12-1961	01°♏35'
11-19-1961	11°♏43'
11-26-1961	22°♏34'
12-03-1961	03°♐32'
12-10-1961	14°♐30'
12-17-1961	25°♐31'
12-24-1961	06°♑38'
12-31-1961	17°♑56'
01-07-1962	29°♑19'
01-14-1962	10°♒19'
01-21-1962	19°♒20'
01-28-1962	22°♒47'Rx
02-04-1962	17°♒52'Rx
02-11-1962	10°♒05'Rx
02-18-1962	07°♒15'
02-25-1962	09°♒55'
03-04-1962	16°♒02'
03-11-1962	24°♒15'
03-18-1962	03°♓54'
03-25-1962	14°♓41'
04-01-1962	26°♓35'
04-08-1962	09°♈37'

Apr 15, 1962 00:00 am EST

Date	☿ Geo Lon
04-15-1962	23°♈45'
04-22-1962	08°♉34'
04-29-1962	22°♉44'
05-06-1962	04°♊43'
05-13-1962	13°♊34'
05-20-1962	18°♊54'
05-27-1962	20°♊22'Rx
06-03-1962	18°♊19'Rx
06-10-1962	14°♊33'Rx
06-17-1962	12°♊00'Rx
06-24-1962	12°♊46'
07-01-1962	17°♊18'
07-08-1962	25°♊22'
07-15-1962	06°♋37'
07-22-1962	20°♋22'
07-29-1962	05°♌07'
08-05-1962	19°♌23'
08-12-1962	02°♍31'
08-19-1962	14°♍25'
08-26-1962	25°♍09'
09-02-1962	04°♎40'
09-09-1962	12°♎46'
09-16-1962	18°♎52'
09-23-1962	21°♎44'
09-30-1962	19°♎32'Rx
10-07-1962	12°♎16'Rx
10-14-1962	06°♎42'Rx
10-21-1962	09°♎09'
10-28-1962	17°♎41'
11-04-1962	28°♎34'
11-11-1962	09°♏56'
11-18-1962	21°♏13'
11-25-1962	02°♐20'
12-02-1962	13°♐20'
12-09-1962	24°♐16'
12-16-1962	05°♑13'
12-23-1962	16°♑05'
12-30-1962	26°♑19'
01-06-1963	04°♒20'
01-13-1963	06°♒25'Rx

Jan 20, 1963 00:00 am EST

Date	☿ Geo Lon
01-20-1963	30°♑00'℞
01-27-1963	22°♑20'℞
02-03-1963	20°♑58'
02-10-1963	24°♑58'
02-17-1963	02°♒00'
02-24-1963	10°♒46'
03-03-1963	20°♒41'
03-10-1963	01°♓35'
03-17-1963	13°♓25'
03-24-1963	26°♓14'
03-31-1963	10°♈03'
04-07-1963	24°♈29'
04-14-1963	08°♉17'
04-21-1963	19°♉38'
04-28-1963	27°♉13'
05-05-1963	00°♊29'
05-12-1963	29°♉32'℞
05-19-1963	25°♉51'℞
05-26-1963	22°♉29'℞
06-02-1963	21°♉57'
06-09-1963	25°♉00'
06-16-1963	01°♊20'
06-23-1963	10°♊33'
06-30-1963	22°♊22'
07-07-1963	06°♋23'
07-14-1963	21°♋25'
07-21-1963	06°♌01'
07-28-1963	19°♌22'
08-04-1963	01°♍20'
08-11-1963	11°♍56'
08-18-1963	21°♍06'
08-25-1963	28°♍33'
09-01-1963	03°♎37'
09-08-1963	05°♎04'℞
09-15-1963	01°♎31'℞
09-22-1963	24°♍27'℞
09-29-1963	20°♍33'℞
10-06-1963	24°♍21'
10-13-1963	03°♎47'
10-20-1963	15°♎23'

Oct 27, 1963 00:00 am EST

Date	☿ Geo Lon
10-27-1963	27°♎17'
11-03-1963	08°♏54'
11-10-1963	20°♏10'
11-17-1963	01°♐10'
11-24-1963	11°♐57'
12-01-1963	22°♐34'
12-08-1963	02°♑53'
12-15-1963	12°♑20'
12-22-1963	19°♑16'
12-29-1963	19°♑59'℞
01-05-1964	12°♑25'℞
01-12-1964	05°♑19'℞
01-19-1964	05°♑23'
01-26-1964	10°♑35'
02-02-1964	18°♑24'
02-09-1964	27°♑38'
02-16-1964	07°♒47'
02-23-1964	18°♒43'
03-01-1964	00°♓27'
03-08-1964	13°♓01'
03-15-1964	26°♓27'
03-22-1964	10°♈26'
03-29-1964	23°♈44'
04-05-1964	04°♉19'
04-12-1964	10°♉22'
04-19-1964	11°♉16'℞
04-26-1964	07°♉58'℞
05-03-1964	03°♉35'℞
05-10-1964	01°♉32'℞
05-17-1964	03°♉09'
05-24-1964	08°♉08'
05-31-1964	15°♉52'
06-07-1964	25°♉57'
06-14-1964	08°♊13'
06-21-1964	22°♊24'
06-28-1964	07°♋37'
07-05-1964	22°♋27'
07-12-1964	05°♌57'
07-19-1964	17°♌54'
07-26-1964	28°♌17'

Aug 02, 1964 00:00 am EST

Date	☿ Geo Lon
08-02-1964	06°♍59'
08-09-1964	13°♍37'
08-16-1964	17°♍27'
08-23-1964	17°♍20'℞
08-30-1964	12°♍44'℞
09-06-1964	06°♍27'℞
09-13-1964	04°♍27'
09-20-1964	09°♍35'
09-27-1964	19°♍52'
10-04-1964	02°♎09'
10-11-1964	14°♎34'
10-18-1964	26°♎32'
10-25-1964	07°♏59'
11-01-1964	18°♏59'
11-08-1964	29°♏37'
11-15-1964	09°♐55'
11-22-1964	19°♐41'
11-29-1964	28°♐19'
12-06-1964	04°♑07'
12-13-1964	03°♑28'℞
12-20-1964	25°♐08'℞
12-27-1964	18°♐52'℞
01-03-1965	20°♐21'
01-10-1965	26°♐38'
01-17-1965	05°♑08'
01-24-1965	14°♑46'
01-31-1965	25°♑07'
02-07-1965	06°♒04'
02-14-1965	17°♒39'
02-21-1965	29°♒57'
02-28-1965	12°♓58'
03-07-1965	26°♓25'
03-14-1965	09°♈09'
03-21-1965	18°♈49'
03-28-1965	23°♈08'
04-04-1965	21°♈32'℞
04-11-1965	16°♈27'℞
04-18-1965	12°♈25'℞
04-25-1965	12°♈08'
05-02-1965	15°♈39'

May 09, 1965 00:00 am EST

Date	☿ Geo Lon
05-09-1965	22°♈08'
05-16-1965	00°♉54'
05-23-1965	11°♉37'
05-30-1965	24°♉11'
06-06-1965	08°♊27'
06-13-1965	23°♊44'
06-20-1965	08°♋42'
06-27-1965	22°♋16'
07-04-1965	04°♌06'
07-11-1965	14°♌07'
07-18-1965	22°♌08'
07-25-1965	27°♌43'
08-01-1965	00°♍04'
08-08-1965	28°♌22'℞
08-15-1965	23°♌13'℞
08-22-1965	18°♌22'℞
08-29-1965	18°♌27'
09-05-1965	24°♌52'
09-12-1965	05°♍55'
09-19-1965	18°♍49'
09-26-1965	01°♎45'
10-03-1965	14°♎05'
10-10-1965	25°♎43'
10-17-1965	06°♏45'
10-24-1965	17°♏15'
10-31-1965	27°♏13'
11-07-1965	06°♐25'
11-14-1965	14°♐12'
11-21-1965	18°♐48'
11-28-1965	16°♐48'℞
12-05-1965	08°♐02'℞
12-12-1965	02°♐51'℞
12-19-1965	05°♐39'
12-26-1965	12°♐56'
01-02-1966	22°♐06'
01-09-1966	02°♑06'
01-16-1966	12°♑37'
01-23-1966	23°♑35'
01-30-1966	05°♒01'
02-06-1966	17°♒01'

Feb 13, 1966 00:00 am EST

☿

Date	Geo Lon
02-13-1966	29°≈36'
02-20-1966	12°⨯28'
02-27-1966	24°⨯31'
03-06-1966	03°♈12'
03-13-1966	05°♈39'℞
03-20-1966	01°♈41'℞
03-27-1966	25°⨯42'℞
04-03-1966	22°⨯47'℞
04-10-1966	24°⨯18'
04-17-1966	29°⨯21'
04-24-1966	06°♈56'
05-01-1966	16°♈26'
05-08-1966	27°♈34'
05-15-1966	10°♉17'
05-22-1966	24°♉32'
05-29-1966	09°♊47'
06-05-1966	24°♊47'
06-12-1966	08°♋18'
06-19-1966	19°♋52'
06-26-1966	29°♋19'
07-03-1966	06°♌23'
07-10-1966	10°♌35'
07-17-1966	11°♌12'℞
07-24-1966	08°♌06'℞
07-31-1966	03°♌12'℞
08-07-1966	00°♌22'℞
08-14-1966	02°♌33'
08-21-1966	10°♌11'
08-28-1966	21°♌55'
09-04-1966	05°♍24'
09-11-1966	18°♍50'
09-18-1966	01°♎31'
09-25-1966	13°♎21'
10-02-1966	24°♎25'
10-09-1966	04°♏47'
10-16-1966	14°♏25'
10-23-1966	23°♏02'
10-30-1966	29°♏55'
11-06-1966	03°♐14'
11-13-1966	29°♏56'℞

Nov 20, 1966 00:00 am EST

☿

Date	Geo Lon
11-20-1966	21°♏07'℞
11-27-1966	17°♏08'
12-04-1966	21°♏12'
12-11-1966	29°♏25'
12-18-1966	09°♐12'
12-25-1966	19°♐35'
01-01-1967	00°♑16'
01-08-1967	11°♑14'
01-15-1967	22°♑31'
01-22-1967	04°≈13'
01-29-1967	16°≈20'
02-05-1967	28°≈36'
02-12-1967	09°⨯53'
02-19-1967	17°⨯30'
02-26-1967	18°⨯04'℞
03-05-1967	12°⨯07'℞
03-12-1967	06°⨯04'℞
03-19-1967	04°⨯40'
03-26-1967	07°⨯48'
04-02-1967	14°⨯03'
04-09-1967	22°⨯25'
04-16-1967	02°♈24'
04-23-1967	13°♈48'
04-30-1967	26°♈33'
05-07-1967	10°♉41'
05-14-1967	25°♉47'
05-21-1967	10°♊43'
05-28-1967	24°♊05'
06-04-1967	05°♋11'
06-11-1967	13°♋46'
06-18-1967	19°♋32'
06-25-1967	21°♋56'
07-02-1967	20°♋42'℞
07-09-1967	16°♋47'℞
07-16-1967	13°♋03'℞
07-23-1967	12°♋36'
07-30-1967	16°♋48'
08-06-1967	25°♋33'
08-13-1967	07°♌52'
08-20-1967	21°♌52'

Aug 27, 1967 00:00 am EST

	☿
Date	Geo Lon
08-27-1967	05°♍46'
09-03-1967	18°♍48'
09-10-1967	00°♎50'
09-17-1967	11°♎56'
09-24-1967	22°♎10'
10-01-1967	01°♏26'
10-08-1967	09°♏26'
10-15-1967	15°♏19'
10-22-1967	17°♏17'Rx
10-29-1967	12°♏47'Rx
11-05-1967	04°♏17'Rx
11-12-1967	01°♏39'
11-19-1967	06°♏55'
11-26-1967	16°♏01'
12-03-1967	26°♏24'
12-10-1967	07°♐08'
12-17-1967	18°♐00'
12-24-1967	28°♐59'
12-31-1967	10°♑08'
01-07-1968	21°♑32'
01-14-1968	03°♒11'
01-21-1968	14°♒48'
01-28-1968	25°♒16'
02-04-1968	01°♓44'
02-11-1968	00°♓28'Rx
02-18-1968	23°♒05'Rx
02-25-1968	17°♒40'Rx
03-03-1968	17°♒51'
03-10-1968	22°♒21'
03-17-1968	29°♒31'
03-24-1968	08°♓29'
03-31-1968	18°♓47'
04-07-1968	00°♈17'
04-14-1968	13°♈00'
04-21-1968	26°♈56'
04-28-1968	11°♉48'
05-05-1968	26°♉32'
05-12-1968	09°♊36'
05-19-1968	20°♊02'
05-26-1968	27°♊25'

Jun 02, 1968 00:00 am EST

	☿
Date	Geo Lon
06-02-1968	01°♋25'
06-09-1968	01°♋42'Rx
06-16-1968	28°♊49'Rx
06-23-1968	25°♊01'Rx
06-30-1968	23°♊15'Rx
07-07-1968	25°♊14'
07-14-1968	01°♋15'
07-21-1968	11°♋00'
07-28-1968	23°♋49'
08-04-1968	08°♌13'
08-11-1968	22°♌33'
08-18-1968	05°♍55'
08-25-1968	18°♍08'
09-01-1968	29°♍15'
09-08-1968	09°♎18'
09-15-1968	18°♎10'
09-22-1968	25°♎28'
09-29-1968	00°♏16'
10-06-1968	00°♏48'Rx
10-13-1968	25°♎17'Rx
10-20-1968	17°♎30'Rx
10-27-1968	16°♎19'
11-03-1968	22°♎42'
11-10-1968	02°♏39'
11-17-1968	13°♏37'
11-24-1968	24°♏44'
12-01-1968	05°♐48'
12-08-1968	16°♐47'
12-15-1968	27°♐49'
12-22-1968	08°♑56'
12-29-1968	20°♑07'
01-05-1969	01°♒03'
01-12-1969	10°♒38'
01-19-1969	15°♒54'
01-26-1969	12°♒57'Rx
02-02-1969	04°♒42'Rx
02-09-1969	00°♒20'Rx
02-16-1969	02°♒03'
02-23-1969	07°♒41'
03-02-1969	15°♒36'

Mar 09, 1969 00:00 am EST

Date	☿ Geo Lon
03-09-1969	24°≈59'
03-16-1969	05°✕29'
03-23-1969	17°✕01'
03-30-1969	29°✕37'
04-06-1969	13°♈17'
04-13-1969	27°♈49'
04-20-1969	12°♉15'
04-27-1969	24°♉53'
05-04-1969	04°♊26'
05-11-1969	10°♊14'
05-18-1969	12°♊01'Rx
05-25-1969	10°♊05'Rx
06-01-1969	06°♊18'Rx
06-08-1969	03°♊39'Rx
06-15-1969	04°♊12'
06-22-1969	08°♊24'
06-29-1969	15°♊58'
07-06-1969	26°♊33'
07-13-1969	09°♋45'
07-20-1969	24°♋29'
07-27-1969	09°♌11'
08-03-1969	22°♌50'
08-10-1969	05°♍11'
08-17-1969	16°♍17'
08-24-1969	26°♍07'
08-31-1969	04°♎31'
09-07-1969	11°♎00'
09-14-1969	14°♎35'
09-21-1969	13°♎37'Rx
09-28-1969	07°♎24'Rx
10-05-1969	00°♎46'Rx
10-12-1969	01°♎06'
10-19-1969	08°♎32'
10-26-1969	19°♎16'
11-02-1969	00°♏50'
11-09-1969	12°♏21'
11-16-1969	23°♏36'
11-23-1969	04°♐39'
11-30-1969	15°♐33'
12-07-1969	26°♐23'

Dec 14, 1969 00:00 am EST

Date	☿ Geo Lon
12-14-1969	07°♑06'
12-21-1969	17°♑21'
12-28-1969	25°♑59'
01-04-1970	00°≈00'
01-11-1970	25°♑34'Rx
01-18-1970	16°♑58'Rx
01-25-1970	13°♑53'
02-01-1970	16°♑59'
02-08-1970	23°♑37'
02-15-1970	02°≈09'
02-22-1970	11°≈51'
03-01-1970	22°≈29'
03-08-1970	03°✕59'
03-15-1970	16°✕24'
03-22-1970	29°✕45'
03-29-1970	13°♈53'
04-05-1970	27°♈54'
04-12-1970	09°♉59'
04-19-1970	18°♉24'
04-26-1970	22°♉15'
05-03-1970	21°♉32'Rx
05-10-1970	17°♉46'Rx
05-17-1970	14°♉08'Rx
05-24-1970	13°♉20'
05-31-1970	16°♉09'
06-07-1970	22°♉11'
06-14-1970	00°♊58'
06-21-1970	12°♊13'
06-28-1970	25°♊42'
07-05-1970	10°♋39'
07-12-1970	25°♋38'
07-19-1970	09°♌31'
07-26-1970	21°♌58'
08-02-1970	02°♍58'
08-09-1970	12°♍30'
08-16-1970	20°♍18'
08-23-1970	25°♍49'
08-30-1970	28°♍01'
09-06-1970	25°♍35'Rx
09-13-1970	19°♍07'Rx

Sep 20, 1970 00:00 am EST — ☿

Date	Geo Lon
09-20-1970	14°♍02'℞
09-27-1970	15°♍57'
10-04-1970	24°♍22'
10-11-1970	05°♎52'
10-18-1970	18°♎00'
10-25-1970	29°♎55'
11-01-1970	11°♏24'
11-08-1970	22°♏30'
11-15-1970	03°♐18'
11-22-1970	13°♐52'
11-29-1970	24°♐07'
12-06-1970	03°♑40'
12-13-1970	11°♑18'
12-20-1970	14°♑01'℞
12-27-1970	08°♑17'℞
01-03-1971	29°♐49'℞
01-10-1971	28°♐06'
01-17-1971	02°♑29'
01-24-1971	09°♑59'
01-31-1971	19°♑02'
02-07-1971	29°♑01'
02-14-1971	09°♒44'
02-21-1971	21°♒09'
02-28-1971	03°♓21'
03-07-1971	16°♓21'
03-14-1971	00°♈01'
03-21-1971	13°♈31'
03-28-1971	24°♈57'
04-04-1971	02°♉02'
04-11-1971	03°♉39'℞
04-18-1971	00°♉29'℞
04-25-1971	25°♈44'℞
05-02-1971	23°♈13'℞
05-09-1971	24°♈27'
05-16-1971	29°♈09'
05-23-1971	06°♉35'
05-30-1971	16°♉17'
06-06-1971	28°♉01'
06-13-1971	11°♊42'
06-20-1971	26°♊46'

Jun 27, 1971 00:00 am EST — ☿

Date	Geo Lon
06-27-1971	11°♋56'
07-04-1971	25°♋59'
07-11-1971	08°♌26'
07-18-1971	19°♌14'
07-25-1971	28°♌18'
08-01-1971	05°♍20'
08-08-1971	09°♍39'
08-15-1971	10°♍17'℞
08-22-1971	06°♍35'℞
08-29-1971	00°♍30'℞
09-05-1971	27°♌22'℞
09-12-1971	00°♍51'
09-19-1971	10°♍11'
09-26-1971	22°♍23'
10-03-1971	05°♎06'
10-10-1971	17°♎25'
10-17-1971	29°♎08'
10-24-1971	10°♏18'
10-31-1971	21°♏02'
11-07-1971	01°♐19'
11-14-1971	11°♐06'
11-21-1971	19°♐55'
11-28-1971	26°♐30'
12-05-1971	27°♐52'℞
12-12-1971	21°♐06'℞
12-19-1971	13°♐07'℞
12-26-1971	12°♐47'
01-02-1972	18°♐21'
01-09-1972	26°♐38'
01-16-1972	06°♑09'
01-23-1972	16°♑24'
01-30-1972	27°♑10'
02-06-1972	08°♒30'
02-13-1972	20°♒27'
02-20-1972	03°♓04'
02-27-1972	16°♓14'
03-05-1972	29°♓08'
03-12-1972	09°♈46'
03-19-1972	15°♈24'
03-26-1972	14°♈38'℞

Apr 02, 1972 00:00 am EST

Date	☿ Geo Lon
04-02-1972	09°♈27'℞
04-09-1972	04°♈46'℞
04-16-1972	03°♈52'
04-23-1972	06°♈58'
04-30-1972	13°♈07'
05-07-1972	21°♉35'
05-14-1972	01°♉56'
05-21-1972	14°♉00'
05-28-1972	27°♉45'
06-04-1972	12°♊49'
06-11-1972	28°♊04'
06-18-1972	12°♋11'
06-25-1972	24°♋32'
07-02-1972	04°♌59'
07-09-1972	13°♌24'
07-16-1972	19°♌22'
07-23-1972	22°♌14'
07-30-1972	21°♌12'℞
08-06-1972	16°♌40'℞
08-13-1972	11°♌44'℞
08-20-1972	10°♌47'
08-27-1972	15°♌49'
09-03-1972	25°♌59'
09-10-1972	08°♍49'
09-17-1972	22°♍06'
09-24-1972	04°♎49'
10-01-1972	16°♎47'
10-08-1972	28°♎03'
10-15-1972	08°♏41'
10-22-1972	18°♏44'
10-29-1972	28°♏01'
11-05-1972	06°♐04'
11-12-1972	11°♐32'
11-19-1972	11°♐32'℞
11-26-1972	03°♐59'℞
12-03-1972	26°♏48'℞
12-10-1972	27°♏49'
12-17-1972	04°♐28'
12-24-1972	13°♐29'
12-31-1972	23°♐28'

Jan 07, 1973 00:00 am EST

Date	☿ Geo Lon
01-07-1973	03°♑56'
01-14-1973	14°♑46'
01-21-1973	25°♑59'
01-28-1973	07°♒42'
02-04-1973	19°♒55'
02-11-1973	02°♓31'
02-18-1973	14°♓45'
02-25-1973	24°♓31'
03-04-1973	28°♓35'
03-11-1973	25°♓31'℞
03-18-1973	19°♓04'℞
03-25-1973	15°♓14'℞
04-01-1973	16°♓04'
04-08-1973	20°♓42'
04-15-1973	27°♓57'
04-22-1973	07°♈08'
04-29-1973	17°♈54'
05-06-1973	00°♉10'
05-13-1973	13°♉54'
05-20-1973	28°♉52'
05-27-1973	14°♊05'
06-03-1973	28°♊10'
06-10-1973	10°♋16'
06-17-1973	20°♋09'
06-24-1973	27°♋36'
07-01-1973	02°♌11'
07-08-1973	03°♌15'℞
07-15-1973	00°♌41'℞
07-22-1973	26°♋05'℞
07-29-1973	23°♋00'℞
08-05-1973	24°♋21'
08-12-1973	00°♌52'
08-19-1973	11°♌47'
08-26-1973	25°♌10'
09-02-1973	08°♍58'
09-09-1973	22°♍06'
09-16-1973	04°♎19'
09-23-1973	15°♎40'
09-30-1973	26°♎14'
10-07-1973	06°♏00'

Oct 14, 1973 00:00 am EST		Jul 21, 1974 00:00 am EST	
	☿		☿
Date	Geo Lon	Date	Geo Lon
10-14-1973	14°♏47'	07-21-1974	08°♋08'
10-21-1973	22°♏01'	07-28-1974	16°♋00'
10-28-1973	26°♏17'	08-04-1974	27°♋35'
11-04-1973	24°♏53'℞	08-11-1974	11°♌26'
11-11-1973	16°♏52'℞	08-18-1974	25°♌42'
11-18-1973	10°♏44'℞	08-25-1974	09°♍13'
11-25-1973	13°♏04'	09-01-1974	21°♍41'
12-02-1973	20°♏44'	09-08-1974	03°♎07'
12-09-1973	00°♐27'	09-15-1974	13°♎35'
12-16-1973	10°♐52'	09-22-1974	23°♎04'
12-23-1973	21°♐34'	09-29-1974	01°♏18'
12-30-1973	02°♑28'	10-06-1974	07°♏38'
01-06-1974	13°♑36'	10-13-1974	10°♏36'
01-13-1974	25°♑03'	10-20-1974	07°♏51'℞
01-20-1974	06°♒52'	10-27-1974	29°♎43'℞
01-27-1974	18°♒54'	11-03-1974	24°♎52'℞
02-03-1974	00°♓24'	11-10-1974	28°♎28'
02-10-1974	09°♓13'	11-17-1974	07°♏06'
02-17-1974	11°♓40'℞	11-24-1974	17°♏30'
02-24-1974	06°♓33'℞	12-01-1974	28°♏21'
03-03-1974	29°♒38'℞	12-08-1974	09°♐17'
03-10-1974	27°♒09'	12-15-1974	20°♐15'
03-17-1974	29°♒35'	12-22-1974	01°♑18'
03-24-1974	05°♓26'	12-29-1974	12°♑31'
03-31-1974	13°♓30'	01-05-1975	23°♑55'
04-07-1974	23°♓10'	01-12-1975	05°♒22'
04-14-1974	04°♈12'	01-19-1975	16°♒04'
04-21-1974	16°♈31'	01-26-1975	23°♒51'
04-28-1974	00°♉09'	02-02-1975	24°♒44'℞
05-05-1974	14°♉56'	02-09-1975	17°♒57'℞
05-12-1974	00°♊00'	02-16-1975	11°♒15'℞
05-19-1974	13°♊55'	02-23-1975	10°♒17'
05-26-1974	25°♊37'	03-02-1975	14°♒08'
06-02-1974	04°♋40'	03-09-1975	20°♒57'
06-09-1974	10°♋47'	03-16-1975	29°♒37'
06-16-1974	13°♋32'	03-23-1975	09°♓38'
06-23-1974	12°♋39'℞	03-30-1975	20°♓47'
06-30-1974	09°♋01'℞	04-06-1975	03°♈04'
07-07-1974	05°♋21'℞	04-13-1975	16°♈32'
07-14-1974	04°♋36'	04-20-1975	01°♉02'

Apr 27, 1975 00:00 am EST

Date	☿ Geo Lon
04-27-1975	15°♉51'
05-04-1975	29°♉29'
05-11-1975	10°♊35'
05-18-1975	18°♊29'
05-25-1975	22°♊49'
06-01-1975	23°♊21'℞
06-08-1975	20°♊39'℞
06-15-1975	16°♊54'℞
06-22-1975	15°♊01'℞
06-29-1975	16°♊43'
07-06-1975	22°♊13'
07-13-1975	01°♋15'
07-20-1975	13°♋24'
07-27-1975	27°♋37'
08-03-1975	12°♌17'
08-10-1975	26°♌10'
08-17-1975	08°♍50'
08-24-1975	20°♍20'
08-31-1975	00°♎41'
09-07-1975	09°♎49'
09-14-1975	17°♎26'
09-21-1975	22°♎46'
09-28-1975	24°♎20'℞
10-05-1975	20°♎19'℞
10-12-1975	12°♎29'℞
10-19-1975	09°♎09'
10-26-1975	13°♎57'
11-02-1975	23°♎29'
11-09-1975	04°♏33'
11-16-1975	15°♏52'
11-23-1975	27°♏03'
11-30-1975	08°♐06'
12-07-1975	19°♐04'
12-14-1975	00°♑03'
12-21-1975	11°♑03'
12-28-1975	21°♑53'
01-04-1976	01°♒46'
01-11-1976	08°♒27'
01-18-1976	07°♒48'℞
01-25-1976	29°♑49'℞

Feb 01, 1976 00:00 am EST

Date	☿ Geo Lon
02-01-1976	23°♑50'℞
02-08-1976	24°♑22'
02-15-1976	29°♑26'
02-22-1976	07°♒03'
02-29-1976	16°♒11'
03-07-1976	26°♒26'
03-14-1976	07°♓38'
03-21-1976	19°♓49'
03-28-1976	03°♈02'
04-04-1976	17°♈11'
04-11-1976	01°♉39'
04-18-1976	14°♉53'
04-25-1976	25°♉11'
05-02-1976	01°♊36'
05-09-1976	03°♊44'℞
05-16-1976	01°♊55'℞
05-23-1976	28°♉04'℞
05-30-1976	25°♉15'℞
06-06-1976	25°♉36'
06-13-1976	29°♉31'
06-20-1976	06°♊39'
06-27-1976	16°♊39'
07-04-1976	29°♊14'
07-11-1976	13°♋44'
07-18-1976	28°♋43'
07-25-1976	12°♌54'
08-01-1976	25°♌46'
08-08-1976	07°♍16'
08-15-1976	17°♍26'
08-22-1976	26°♍08'
08-29-1976	03°♎00'
09-05-1976	07°♎12'
09-12-1976	07°♎17'℞
09-19-1976	02°♎13'℞
09-26-1976	25°♍11'℞
10-03-1976	23°♍30'
10-10-1976	29°♍29'
10-17-1976	09°♎51'
10-24-1976	21°♎35'
10-31-1976	03°♏20'

Nov 07, 1976 00:00 am EST ☿

Date	Geo Lon
11-07-1976	14°♏48'
11-14-1976	25°♏57'
11-21-1976	06°♐52'
11-28-1976	17°♐38'
12-05-1976	28°♐14'
12-12-1976	08°♑27'
12-19-1976	17°♑27'
12-26-1976	22°♑58'
01-02-1977	20°♑53'℞
01-09-1977	12°♑10'℞
01-16-1977	07°♑11'℞
01-23-1977	09°♑10'
01-30-1977	15°♑19'
02-06-1977	23°♑36'
02-13-1977	03°≈07'
02-20-1977	13°≈31'
02-27-1977	24°≈44'
03-06-1977	06°♓45'
03-13-1977	19°♓40'
03-20-1977	03°♈25'
03-27-1977	17°♈26'
04-03-1977	00°♉09'
04-10-1977	09°♉29'
04-17-1977	14°♉06'
04-24-1977	13°♉44'℞
05-01-1977	09°♉53'℞
05-08-1977	05°♉54'℞
05-15-1977	04°♉47'
05-22-1977	07°♉19'
05-29-1977	13°♉04'
06-05-1977	21°♉28'
06-12-1977	02°♊13'
06-19-1977	15°♊08'
06-26-1977	29°♊48'
07-03-1977	15°♋01'
07-10-1977	29°♋26'
07-17-1977	12°♌24'
07-24-1977	23°♌51'
07-31-1977	03°♍44'
08-07-1977	11°♍53'

Aug 14, 1977 00:00 am EST ☿

Date	Geo Lon
08-14-1977	17°♍50'
08-21-1977	20°♍41'
08-28-1977	19°♍14'℞
09-04-1977	13°♍33'℞
09-11-1977	07°♍50'℞
09-18-1977	07°♍57'
09-25-1977	15°♍02'
10-02-1977	26°♍12'
10-09-1977	08°♎33'
10-16-1977	20°♎46'
10-23-1977	02°♏31'
10-30-1977	13°♏47'
11-06-1977	24°♏40'
11-13-1977	05°♐13'
11-20-1977	15°♐25'
11-27-1977	25°♐01'
12-04-1977	03°♑06'
12-11-1977	07°♑23'
12-18-1977	03°♑58'℞
12-25-1977	24°♐56'℞
01-01-1978	21°♐09'
01-08-1978	24°♐28'
01-15-1978	01°♑34'
01-22-1978	10°♑27'
01-29-1978	20°♑18'
02-05-1978	00°≈51'
02-12-1978	12°≈01'
02-19-1978	23°≈52'
02-26-1978	06°♓27'
03-05-1978	19°♓45'
03-12-1978	03°♈14'
03-19-1978	15°♈19'
03-26-1978	23°♈34'
04-02-1978	26°♈07'℞
04-09-1978	23°♈14'℞
04-16-1978	18°♈08'℞
04-23-1978	15°♈02'℞
04-30-1978	15°♈50'
05-07-1978	20°♈13'
05-14-1978	27°♈22'

Aug 14, 1977 00:00 am EST

☿

Date	Geo Lon
08-14-1977	17°♍50'
08-21-1977	20°♍41'
08-28-1977	19°♍14'Rx
09-04-1977	13°♍33'Rx
09-11-1977	07°♍50'Rx
09-18-1977	07°♍57'
09-25-1977	15°♍02'
10-02-1977	26°♍12'
10-09-1977	08°♎33'
10-16-1977	20°♎46'
10-23-1977	02°♏31'
10-30-1977	13°♏47'
11-06-1977	24°♏40'
11-13-1977	05°♐13'
11-20-1977	15°♐25'
11-27-1977	25°♐01'
12-04-1977	03°♑06'
12-11-1977	07°♑23'
12-18-1977	03°♑58'Rx
12-25-1977	24°♐56'Rx
01-01-1978	21°♐09'
01-08-1978	24°♐28'
01-15-1978	01°♑34'
01-22-1978	10°♑27'
01-29-1978	20°♑18'
02-05-1978	00°♒51'
02-12-1978	12°♒01'
02-19-1978	23°♒52'
02-26-1978	06°♓27'
03-05-1978	19°♓45'
03-12-1978	03°♈14'
03-19-1978	15°♈19'
03-26-1978	23°♈34'
04-02-1978	26°♈07'Rx
04-09-1978	23°♈14'Rx
04-16-1978	18°♈08'Rx
04-23-1978	15°♈02'Rx
04-30-1978	15°♈50'
05-07-1978	20°♈13'
05-14-1978	27°♈22'

May 21, 1978 00:00 am EST

☿

Date	Geo Lon
05-21-1978	06°♉42'
05-28-1978	17°♉59'
06-04-1978	01°♊08'
06-11-1978	15°♊52'
06-18-1978	01°♋12'
06-25-1978	15°♋45'
07-02-1978	28°♋45'
07-09-1978	10°♌01'
07-16-1978	19°♌28'
07-23-1978	26°♌52'
07-30-1978	01°♍39'
08-06-1978	02°♍57'Rx
08-13-1978	00°♍04'Rx
08-20-1978	24°♌22'Rx
08-27-1978	20°♌29'Rx
09-03-1978	22°♌28'
09-10-1978	00°♍36'
09-17-1978	12°♍28'
09-24-1978	25°♍26'
10-01-1978	08°♎07'
10-08-1978	20°♎10'
10-15-1978	01°♏34'
10-22-1978	12°♏25'
10-29-1978	22°♏46'
11-05-1978	02°♐34'
11-12-1978	11°♐31'
11-19-1978	18°♐38'
11-26-1978	21°♐37'Rx
12-03-1978	16°♐59'Rx
12-10-1978	08°♐02'Rx
12-17-1978	05°♐33'
12-24-1978	10°♐07'
12-31-1978	18°♐06'
01-07-1979	27°♐32'
01-14-1979	07°♑42'
01-21-1979	18°♑21'
01-28-1979	29°♑28'
02-04-1979	11°♒07'
02-11-1979	23°♒22'
02-18-1979	06°♓11'

Feb 25, 1979 00:00 am EST
☿

Date	Geo Lon
02-25-1979	19°♓04'
03-04-1979	00°♈26'
03-11-1979	07°♈27'
03-18-1979	07°♈50'℞
03-25-1979	02°♈47'℞
04-01-1979	27°♓24'℞
04-08-1979	25°♓46'
04-15-1979	28°♓22'
04-22-1979	04°♈12'
04-29-1979	12°♈21'
05-06-1979	22°♈21'
05-13-1979	03°♉59'
05-20-1979	17°♉14'
05-27-1979	01°♊55'
06-03-1979	17°♊16'
06-10-1979	01°♋52'
06-17-1979	14°♋47'
06-24-1979	25°♋42'
07-01-1979	04°♌30'
07-08-1979	10°♌51'
07-15-1979	14°♌09'
07-22-1979	13°♌43'℞
07-29-1979	09°♌46'℞
08-05-1979	04°♌55'℞
08-12-1979	03°♌14'
08-19-1979	07°♌03'
08-26-1979	16°♌10'
09-02-1979	28°♌40'
09-09-1979	12°♍12'
09-16-1979	25°♍21'
09-23-1979	07°♎42'
09-30-1979	19°♎14'
10-07-1979	00°♏04'
10-14-1979	10°♏13'
10-21-1979	19°♏37'
10-28-1979	27°♏53'
11-04-1979	03°♐59'
11-11-1979	05°♐37'℞
11-18-1979	29°♏54'℞
11-25-1979	21°♏25'℞

Dec 02, 1979 00:00 am EST
☿

Date	Geo Lon
12-02-1979	20°♏16'
12-09-1979	26°♏00'
12-16-1979	04°♐48'
12-23-1979	14°♐47'
12-30-1979	25°♐14'
01-06-1980	05°♑59'
01-13-1980	17°♑04'
01-20-1980	28°♑31'
01-27-1980	10°♒25'
02-03-1980	22°♒43'
02-10-1980	04°♓56'
02-17-1980	15°♓30'
02-24-1980	21°♓13'
03-02-1980	19°♓28'℞
03-09-1980	12°♓50'℞
03-16-1980	07°♓59'℞
03-23-1980	08°♓02'
03-30-1980	12°♓09'
04-06-1980	19°♓04'
04-13-1980	27°♓57'
04-20-1980	08°♈22'
04-27-1980	20°♈12'
05-04-1980	03°♉27'
05-11-1980	18°♉01'
05-18-1980	03°♊15'
05-25-1980	17°♊48'
06-01-1980	00°♋29'
06-08-1980	10°♋51'
06-15-1980	18°♋42'
06-22-1980	23°♋38'
06-29-1980	25°♋06'℞
07-06-1980	22°♋58'℞
07-13-1980	18°♋41'℞
07-20-1980	15°♋29'℞
07-27-1980	16°♋12'
08-03-1980	21°♋45'
08-10-1980	01°♌46'
08-17-1980	14°♌49'
08-24-1980	28°♌51'
08-31-1980	12°♍26'

Sep 07, 1980 00:00 am EST

☿

Date	Geo Lon
09-07-1980	25°♍05'
09-14-1980	06°♎47'
09-21-1980	17°♎35'
09-28-1980	27°♎32'
10-05-1980	06°♏30'
10-12-1980	14°♏01'
10-19-1980	19°♏01'
10-26-1980	19°♏14'℞
11-02-1980	12°♏40'℞
11-09-1980	05°♏00'℞
11-16-1980	05°♏12'
11-23-1980	12°♏02'
11-30-1980	21°♏37'
12-07-1980	02°♐06'
12-14-1980	12°♐52'
12-21-1980	23°♐44'
12-28-1980	04°♑46'
01-04-1981	16°♑01'
01-11-1981	27°♑34'
01-18-1981	09°♒21'
01-25-1981	20°♒52'
02-01-1981	00°♓32'
02-08-1981	04°♓55'
02-15-1981	01°♓11'℞
02-22-1981	23°♒39'℞
03-01-1981	19°♒55'℞
03-08-1981	21°♒33'
03-15-1981	26°♒56'
03-22-1981	04°♓41'
03-29-1981	14°♓04'
04-05-1981	24°♓45'
04-12-1981	06°♈40'
04-19-1981	19°♈49'
04-26-1981	04°♉10'
05-03-1981	19°♉11'
05-10-1981	03°♊33'
05-17-1981	15°♊52'
05-24-1981	25°♊26'
05-31-1981	01°♋57'
06-07-1981	05°♋01'

Jun 14, 1981 00:00 am EST

☿

Date	Geo Lon
06-14-1981	04°♋24'℞
06-21-1981	01°♋00'℞
06-28-1981	27°♊24'℞
07-05-1981	26°♊27'
07-12-1981	29°♊29'
07-19-1981	06°♋36'
07-26-1981	17°♋24'
08-02-1981	00°♌54'
08-09-1981	15°♌23'
08-16-1981	29°♌23'
08-23-1981	12°♍18'
08-30-1981	24°♍07'
09-06-1981	04°♎54'
09-13-1981	14°♎36'
09-20-1981	23°♎05'
09-27-1981	29°♎48'
10-04-1981	03°♏36'
10-11-1981	02°♏22'℞
10-18-1981	25°♎14'℞
10-25-1981	18°♎42'℞
11-01-1981	20°♎15'
11-08-1981	28°♎07'
11-15-1981	08°♏29'
11-22-1981	19°♏28'
11-29-1981	00°♐32'
12-06-1981	11°♐33'
12-13-1981	22°♐33'
12-20-1981	03°♑37'
12-27-1981	14°♑49'
01-03-1982	26°♑03'
01-10-1982	06°♒51'
01-17-1982	15°♒33'
01-24-1982	18°♒33'℞
01-31-1982	13°♒07'℞
02-07-1982	05°♒20'℞
02-14-1982	02°♒58'
02-21-1982	06°♒04'
02-28-1982	12°♒28'
03-07-1982	20°♒52'
03-14-1982	00°♓36'

	☿
Date	Geo Lon
06-14-1981	04°♋24'℞
06-21-1981	01°♋00'℞
06-28-1981	27°♊24'℞
07-05-1981	26°♊27'
07-12-1981	29°♊29'
07-19-1981	06°♋36'
07-26-1981	17°♋24'
08-02-1981	00°♌54'
08-09-1981	15°♌23'
08-16-1981	29°♌23'
08-23-1981	12°♍18'
08-30-1981	24°♍07'
09-06-1981	04°♎54'
09-13-1981	14°♎36'
09-20-1981	23°♎05'
09-27-1981	29°♎48'
10-04-1981	03°♏36'
10-11-1981	02°♏22'℞
10-18-1981	25°♎14'℞
10-25-1981	18°♎42'℞
11-01-1981	20°♎15'
11-08-1981	28°♎07'
11-15-1981	08°♏29'
11-22-1981	19°♏28'
11-29-1981	00°♐32'
12-06-1981	11°♐33'
12-13-1981	22°♐33'
12-20-1981	03°♑37'
12-27-1981	14°♑49'
01-03-1982	26°♑03'
01-10-1982	06°♒51'
01-17-1982	15°♒33'
01-24-1982	18°♒33'℞
01-31-1982	13°♒07'℞
02-07-1982	05°♒20'℞
02-14-1982	02°♒58'
02-21-1982	06°♒04'
02-28-1982	12°♒28'
03-07-1982	20°♒52'
03-14-1982	00°♓36'

Mar 21, 1982 00:00 am EST

	☿
Date	Geo Lon
03-21-1982	11°♓27'
03-28-1982	23°♓20'
04-04-1982	06°♈20'
04-11-1982	20°♈23'
04-18-1982	05°♉06'
04-25-1982	19°♉10'
05-02-1982	00°♊58'
05-09-1982	09°♊28'
05-16-1982	14°♊13'
05-23-1982	15°♊00'℞
05-30-1982	12°♊25'℞
06-06-1982	08°♊38'℞
06-13-1982	06°♊38'℞
06-20-1982	08°♊06'
06-27-1982	13°♊12'
07-04-1982	21°♊38'
07-11-1982	03°♋05'
07-18-1982	16°♋56'
07-25-1982	01°♌47'
08-01-1982	16°♌08'
08-08-1982	29°♌19'
08-15-1982	11°♍14'
08-22-1982	21°♍56'
08-29-1982	01°♎21'
09-05-1982	09°♎16'
09-12-1982	15°♎04'
09-19-1982	17°♎31'
09-26-1982	14°♎53'℞
10-03-1982	07°♎36'℞
10-10-1982	02°♎31'℞
10-17-1982	05°♎25'
10-24-1982	14°♎15'
10-31-1982	25°♎20'
11-07-1982	06°♏51'
11-14-1982	18°♏13'
11-21-1982	29°♏23'
11-28-1982	10°♐22'
12-05-1982	21°♐16'
12-12-1982	02°♑07'
12-19-1982	12°♑50'

Jun 14, 1981 00:00 am EST

Dec 26, 1982 00:00 am EST

Date	☿ Geo Lon
12-26-1982	22°♑51'
01-02-1983	00°≈32'
01-09-1983	02°≈09'℞
01-16-1983	25°♑20'℞
01-23-1983	17°♑50'℞
01-30-1983	16°♑55'
02-06-1983	21°♑18'
02-13-1983	28°♑35'
02-20-1983	07°≈29'
02-27-1983	17°≈30'
03-06-1983	28°≈25'
03-13-1983	10°♓13'
03-20-1983	23°♓00'
03-27-1983	06°♈43'
04-03-1983	21°♈01'
04-10-1983	04°♉41'
04-17-1983	15°♉48'
04-24-1983	22°♉57'
05-01-1983	25°♉32'
05-08-1983	23°♉52'℞
05-15-1983	19°♉53'℞
05-22-1983	16°♉49'℞
05-29-1983	16°♉56'
06-05-1983	20°♉35'
06-12-1983	27°♉23'
06-19-1983	06°♊53'
06-26-1983	18°♊52'
07-03-1983	02°♋57'
07-10-1983	18°♋03'
07-17-1983	02°♌43'
07-24-1983	16°♌06'
07-31-1983	28°♌03'
08-07-1983	08°♍36'
08-14-1983	17°♍38'
08-21-1983	24°♍52'
08-28-1983	29°♍35'
09-04-1983	00°♎34'℞
09-11-1983	26°♍39'℞
09-18-1983	19°♍44'℞
09-25-1983	16°♍23'

Oct 02, 1983 00:00 am EST

Date	☿ Geo Lon
10-02-1983	20°♍38'
10-09-1983	00°♎21'
10-16-1983	12°♎09'
10-23-1983	24°♎11'
10-30-1983	05°♏53'
11-06-1983	17°♏12'
11-13-1983	28°♏12'
11-20-1983	08°♐57'
11-27-1983	19°♐28'
12-04-1983	29°♐38'
12-11-1983	08°♑51'
12-18-1983	15°♑26'
12-25-1983	15°♑42'℞
01-01-1984	07°♑50'℞
01-08-1984	01°♑00'℞
01-15-1984	01°♑31'
01-22-1984	07°♑04'
01-29-1984	15°♑06'
02-05-1984	24°♑27'
02-12-1984	04°≈40'
02-19-1984	15°≈37'
02-26-1984	27°≈19'
03-04-1984	09°♓49'
03-11-1984	23°♓09'
03-18-1984	06°♈59'
03-25-1984	20°♈07'
04-01-1984	00°♉25'
04-08-1984	05°♉58'
04-15-1984	06°♉08'℞
04-22-1984	02°♉14'℞
04-29-1984	27°♈52'℞
05-06-1984	26°♈19'
05-13-1984	28°♈31'
05-20-1984	03°♉59'
05-27-1984	12°♉04'
06-03-1984	22°♉22'
06-10-1984	04°♊45'
06-17-1984	18°♊59'
06-24-1984	04°♋14'
07-01-1984	19°♋06'

Jul 08, 1984 00:00 am EST ☿	
Date	Geo Lon
07-08-1984	02°♌37'
07-15-1984	14°♌32'
07-22-1984	24°♌49'
07-29-1984	03°♍20'
08-05-1984	09°♍41'
08-12-1984	13°♍06'
08-19-1984	12°♍30'Rx
08-26-1984	07°♍39'Rx
09-02-1984	01°♍43'Rx
09-09-1984	00°♍20'
09-16-1984	05°♍53'
09-23-1984	16°♍25'
09-30-1984	28°♍53'
10-07-1984	11°♎27'
10-14-1984	23°♎30'
10-21-1984	05°♏00'
10-28-1984	16°♏00'
11-04-1984	26°♏36'
11-11-1984	06°♐48'
11-18-1984	16°♐24'
11-25-1984	24°♐48'
12-02-1984	00°♑14'
12-09-1984	29°♐07'Rx
12-16-1984	20°♐36'Rx
12-23-1984	14°♐41'Rx
12-30-1984	16°♐36'
01-06-1985	23°♐11'
01-13-1985	01°♑54'
01-20-1985	11°♑39'
01-27-1985	22°♑03'
02-03-1985	03°♒01'
02-10-1985	14°♒34'
02-17-1985	26°♒47'
02-24-1985	09°♓41'
03-03-1985	22°♓59'
03-10-1985	05°♈31'
03-17-1985	14°♈53'
03-24-1985	18°♈38'
03-31-1985	16°♈18'Rx
04-07-1985	10°♈52'Rx

Apr 14, 1985 00:00 am EST ☿	
Date	Geo Lon
04-14-1985	07°♈07'Rx
04-21-1985	07°♈23'
04-28-1985	11°♈24'
05-05-1985	18°♈14'
05-12-1985	27°♈15'
05-19-1985	08°♉07'
05-26-1985	20°♉45'
06-02-1985	05°♊02'
06-09-1985	20°♊19'
06-16-1985	05°♋18'
06-23-1985	18°♋51'
06-30-1985	00°♌37'
07-07-1985	10°♌28'
07-14-1985	18°♌15'
07-21-1985	23°♌27'
07-28-1985	25°♌19'Rx
08-04-1985	23°♌09'Rx
08-11-1985	17°♌58'Rx
08-18-1985	13°♌40'Rx
08-25-1985	14°♌23'
09-01-1985	21°♌11'
09-08-1985	02°♍28'
09-15-1985	15°♍33'
09-22-1985	28°♍37'
09-29-1985	11°♎02'
10-06-1985	22°♎43'
10-13-1985	03°♏45'
10-20-1985	14°♏13'
10-27-1985	24°♏05'
11-03-1985	03°♐07'
11-10-1985	10°♐38'
11-17-1985	14°♐51'
11-24-1985	12°♐24'Rx
12-01-1985	03°♐34'Rx
12-08-1985	28°♏46'Rx
12-15-1985	02°♐00'
12-22-1985	09°♐34'
12-29-1985	18°♐55'
01-05-1986	29°♐02'
01-12-1986	09°♑36'

Jan 19, 1986 00:00 am EST

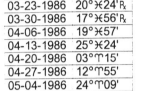
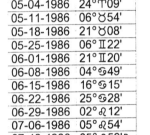

Date	Geo Lon
01-19-1986	20°♑34'
01-26-1986	01°♒58'
02-02-1986	13°♒53'
02-09-1986	26°♒20'
02-16-1986	09°♓03'
02-23-1986	20°♓53'
03-02-1986	29°♓13'
03-09-1986	01°♈05'℞
03-16-1986	26°♓29'℞
03-23-1986	20°♓24'℞
03-30-1986	17°♓56'℞
04-06-1986	19°♓57'
04-13-1986	25°♓24'
04-20-1986	03°♈15'
04-27-1986	12°♈55'
05-04-1986	24°♈09'
05-11-1986	06°♉54'
05-18-1986	21°♉08'
05-25-1986	06°♊22'
06-01-1986	21°♊20'
06-08-1986	04°♋49'
06-15-1986	16°♋15'
06-22-1986	25°♋28'
06-29-1986	02°♌12'
07-06-1986	05°♌54'
07-13-1986	05°♌59'℞
07-20-1986	02°♌33'℞
07-27-1986	27°♋53'℞
08-03-1986	25°♋44'
08-10-1986	28°♋32'
08-17-1986	06°♌32'
08-24-1986	18°♌27'
08-31-1986	02°♍06'
09-07-1986	15°♍40'
09-14-1986	28°♍26'
09-21-1986	10°♎19'
09-28-1986	21°♎23'
10-05-1986	01°♏43'
10-12-1986	11°♏14'
10-19-1986	19°♏41'

Oct 25, 1986 00:00 am EST

☿

Date	Geo Lon
10-25-1986	25°♏29'
11-01-1986	29°♏05'
11-08-1986	26°♏27'℞
11-15-1986	17°♏51'℞
11-22-1986	13°♏05'℞
11-29-1986	16°♏38'
12-06-1986	24°♏46'
12-13-1986	04°♐35'
12-20-1986	15°♐01'
12-27-1986	25°♐43'
01-03-1987	06°♑39'
01-10-1987	17°♑52'
01-17-1987	29°♑26'
01-24-1987	11°♒22'
01-31-1987	23°♒29'
02-07-1987	04°♓48'
02-14-1987	12°♓50'
02-21-1987	13°♓57'℞
02-28-1987	08°♓05'℞
03-07-1987	01°♓42'℞
03-14-1987	00°♓02'
03-21-1987	03°♓03'
03-28-1987	09°♓16'
04-04-1987	17°♓35'
04-11-1987	27°♓29'
04-18-1987	08°♈44'
04-25-1987	21°♈19'
05-02-1987	05°♉14'
05-09-1987	20°♉12'
05-16-1987	05°♊11'
05-23-1987	18°♊46'
05-30-1987	00°♋02'
06-06-1987	08°♋42'
06-13-1987	14°♋26'
06-20-1987	16°♋47'
06-27-1987	15°♋30'℞
07-04-1987	11°♋39'℞
07-11-1987	08°♋06'℞
07-18-1987	07°♋47'
07-25-1987	11°♋54'

Aug 01, 1987 00:00 am EST

Date	☿ Geo Lon
08-01-1987	20°♋24'
08-08-1987	02°♌29'
08-15-1987	16°♌30'
08-22-1987	00°♍36'
08-29-1987	13°♍52'
09-05-1987	26°♍05'
09-12-1987	07°♎20'
09-19-1987	17°♎38'
09-26-1987	26°♎56'
10-03-1987	04°♏58'
10-10-1987	10°♏57'
10-17-1987	13°♏12'℞
10-24-1987	09°♏18'℞
10-31-1987	00°♏53'℞
11-07-1987	27°♎28'
11-14-1987	02°♏14'
11-21-1987	11°♏16'
11-28-1987	21°♏44'
12-05-1987	02°♐33'
12-12-1987	13°♐28'
12-19-1987	24°♐26'
12-26-1987	05°♑31'
01-02-1988	16°♑49'
01-09-1988	28°♑19'
01-16-1988	09°♒48'
01-23-1988	20°♒18'
01-30-1988	27°♒14'
02-06-1988	26°♒38'℞
02-13-1988	19°♒17'℞
02-20-1988	13°♒25'℞
02-27-1988	13°♒19'
03-05-1988	17°♒42'
03-12-1988	24°♒49'
03-19-1988	03°♓43'
03-26-1988	13°♓55'
04-02-1988	25°♓17'
04-09-1988	07°♈49'
04-16-1988	21°♈32'
04-23-1988	06°♉14'
04-30-1988	21°♉00'

May 07, 1988 00:00 am EST

Date	☿ Geo Lon
05-07-1988	04°♊16'
05-14-1988	14°♊53'
05-21-1988	22°♊20'
05-28-1988	26°♊15'
06-04-1988	26°♊24'℞
06-11-1988	23°♊27'℞
06-18-1988	19°♊44'℞
06-25-1988	18°♊09'
07-02-1988	20°♊15'
07-09-1988	26°♊14'
07-16-1988	05°♋47'
07-23-1988	18°♋22'
07-30-1988	02°♌46'
08-06-1988	17°♌18'
08-13-1988	00°♍54'
08-20-1988	13°♍19'
08-27-1988	24°♍35'
09-03-1988	04°♎44'
09-10-1988	13°♎39'
09-17-1988	21°♎01'
09-24-1988	25°♎55'
10-01-1988	26°♎45'℞
10-08-1988	21°♎44'℞
10-15-1988	13°♎56'℞
10-22-1988	12°♎00'
10-29-1988	17°♎55'
11-05-1988	27°♎48'
11-12-1988	08°♏53'
11-19-1988	20°♏07'
11-26-1988	01°♐15'
12-03-1988	12°♐16'
12-10-1988	23°♐15'
12-17-1988	04°♑17'
12-24-1988	15°♑20'
12-31-1988	26°♑10'
01-07-1989	05°♒48'
01-14-1989	11°♒34'
01-21-1989	09°♒23'℞
01-28-1989	01°♒03'℞
02-04-1989	26°♑09'℞

Feb 11, 1989 00:00 am EST

Date	☿ Geo Lon
02-11-1989	27°♑34'
02-18-1989	03°♒06'
02-25-1989	10°♒58'
03-04-1989	20°♒17'
03-11-1989	00°♓42'
03-18-1989	12°♓06'
03-25-1989	24°♓30'
04-01-1989	07°♈57'
04-08-1989	22°♈19'
04-15-1989	06°♉44'
04-22-1989	19°♉35'
04-29-1989	29°♉19'
05-06-1989	05°♊10'
05-13-1989	06°♊50'Rx
05-20-1989	04°♊43'Rx
05-27-1989	00°♊52'Rx
06-03-1989	28°♉19'Rx
06-10-1989	29°♉03'
06-17-1989	03°♊20'
06-24-1989	10°♊51'
07-01-1989	21°♊16'
07-08-1989	04°♋16'
07-15-1989	18°♋58'
07-22-1989	03°♌49'
07-29-1989	17°♌43'
08-05-1989	00°♍17'
08-12-1989	11°♍33'
08-19-1989	21°♍29'
08-26-1989	29°♍57'
09-02-1989	06°♎30'
09-09-1989	10°♎13'
09-16-1989	09°♎32'Rx
09-23-1989	03°♎43'Rx
09-30-1989	26°♍58'Rx
10-07-1989	26°♍38'
10-14-1989	03°♎38'
10-21-1989	14°♎20'
10-28-1989	26°♎02'
11-04-1989	07°♏41'
11-11-1989	19°♏02'

Nov 18, 1989 00:00 am EST

Date	☿ Geo Lon
11-18-1989	00°♐07'
11-25-1989	11°♐01'
12-02-1989	21°♐48'
12-09-1989	02°♑25'
12-16-1989	12°♑35'
12-23-1989	21°♑18'
12-30-1989	25°♑50'
01-06-1990	22°♑11'Rx
01-13-1990	13°♑24'Rx
01-20-1990	09°♑42'
01-27-1990	12°♑31'
02-03-1990	19°♑04'
02-10-1990	27°♑33'
02-17-1990	07°♒13'
02-24-1990	17°♒46'
03-03-1990	29°♒08'
03-10-1990	11°♓22'
03-17-1990	24°♓31'
03-24-1990	08°♈27'
03-31-1990	22°♈26'
04-07-1990	04°♉44'
04-14-1990	13°♉24'
04-21-1990	17°♉19'
04-28-1990	16°♉28'Rx
05-05-1990	12°♉30'Rx
05-12-1990	08°♉48'Rx
05-19-1990	08°♉05'
05-26-1990	11°♉00'
06-02-1990	17°♉05'
06-09-1990	25°♉49'
06-16-1990	06°♊55'
06-23-1990	20°♊13'
06-30-1990	05°♋05'
07-07-1990	20°♋12'
07-14-1990	04°♌19'
07-21-1990	16°♌59'
07-28-1990	28°♌09'
08-04-1990	07°♍47'
08-11-1990	15°♍39'
08-18-1990	21°♍14'

Aug 25, 1990 00:00 am EST

☿

Date	Geo Lon
08-25-1990	23°♍34'
09-01-1990	21°♍24'Rx
09-08-1990	15°♍13'Rx
09-15-1990	10°♍00'Rx
09-22-1990	11°♍20'
09-29-1990	19°♍21'
10-06-1990	00°♎49'
10-13-1990	13°♎07'
10-20-1990	25°♎12'
10-27-1990	06°♏48'
11-03-1990	17°♏58'
11-10-1990	28°♏47'
11-17-1990	09°♐19'
11-24-1990	19°♐30'
12-01-1990	29°♐00'
12-08-1990	06°♑44'
12-15-1990	10°♑00'Rx
12-22-1990	05°♑03'Rx
12-29-1990	26°♐15'Rx
01-05-1991	23°♐52'
01-12-1991	27°♐59'
01-19-1991	05°♑25'
01-26-1991	14°♑28'
02-02-1991	24°♑25'
02-09-1991	05°♒04'
02-16-1991	16°♒23'
02-23-1991	28°♒24'
03-02-1991	11°♓12'
03-09-1991	24°♓40'
03-16-1991	08°♈08'
03-23-1991	19°♈46'
03-30-1991	27°♈11'
04-06-1991	28°♈54'Rx
04-13-1991	25°♈35'Rx
04-20-1991	20°♈39'Rx
04-27-1991	18°♈03'Rx
05-04-1991	19°♈19'
05-11-1991	24°♈04'
05-18-1991	01°♉31'
05-25-1991	11°♉08'

Jun 01, 1991 00:00 am EST

☿

Date	Geo Lon
06-01-1991	22°♉44'
06-08-1991	06°♊12'
06-15-1991	21°♊09'
06-22-1991	06°♋26'
06-29-1991	20°♋42'
07-06-1991	03°♌22'
07-13-1991	14°♌20'
07-20-1991	23°♌29'
07-27-1991	00°♍34'
08-03-1991	04°♍57'
08-10-1991	05°♍41'Rx
08-17-1991	02°♍12'Rx
08-24-1991	26°♌20'Rx
08-31-1991	23°♌04'Rx
09-07-1991	26°♌06'
09-14-1991	05°♍04'
09-21-1991	17°♍14'
09-28-1991	00°♎07'
10-05-1991	12°♎38'
10-12-1991	24°♎30'
10-19-1991	05°♏46'
10-26-1991	16°♏32'
11-02-1991	26°♏49'
11-09-1991	06°♐33'
11-16-1991	15°♐21'
11-23-1991	22°♐04'
11-30-1991	24°♐00'Rx
12-07-1991	17°♐57'Rx
12-14-1991	09°♐31'Rx
12-21-1991	08°♐29'
12-28-1991	13°♐48'
01-04-1992	22°♐03'
01-11-1992	01°♑36'
01-18-1992	11°♑50'
01-25-1992	22°♑33'
02-01-1992	03°♒47'
02-08-1992	15°♒35'
02-15-1992	28°♒01'
02-22-1992	10°♓59'
02-29-1992	23°♓50'

Mar 07, 1992 00:00 am EST

Date	☿ Geo Lon
03-07-1992	04°♈43'
03-14-1992	10°♈45'
03-21-1992	10°♈10'℞
03-28-1992	04°♈50'℞
04-04-1992	29°♓54'℞
04-11-1992	28°♓54'
04-18-1992	01°♈59'
04-25-1992	08°♈08'
05-02-1992	16°♈34'
05-09-1992	26°♈49'
05-16-1992	08°♉44'
05-23-1992	22°♉17'
05-30-1992	07°♊13'
06-06-1992	22°♊31'
06-13-1992	06°♋51'
06-20-1992	19°♋24'
06-27-1992	29°♋59'
07-04-1992	08°♌28'
07-11-1992	14°♌28'
07-18-1992	17°♌20'
07-25-1992	16°♌23'℞
08-01-1992	12°♌02'℞
08-08-1992	07°♌16'℞
08-15-1992	06°♌14'
08-22-1992	10°♌56'
08-29-1992	20°♌46'
09-05-1992	03°♍34'
09-12-1992	17°♍01'
09-19-1992	29°♍57'
09-26-1992	12°♎05'
10-03-1992	23°♎28'
10-10-1992	04°♏11'
10-17-1992	14°♏14'
10-24-1992	23°♏31'
10-31-1992	01°♐35'
11-07-1992	07°♐12'
11-14-1992	07°♐46'℞
11-21-1992	00°♐50'℞
11-28-1992	23°♏06'℞
12-05-1992	23°♏25'

Dec 12, 1992 00:00 am EST

Date	☿ Geo Lon
12-12-1992	29°♏51'
12-19-1992	08°♐52'
12-26-1992	18°♐54'
01-02-1993	29°♐23'
01-09-1993	10°♑11'
01-16-1993	21°♑20'
01-23-1993	02°♒54'
01-30-1993	14°♒57'
02-06-1993	27°♒23'
02-13-1993	09°♓33'
02-20-1993	19°♓35'
02-27-1993	24°♓10'
03-06-1993	21°♓21'℞
03-13-1993	14°♓41'℞
03-20-1993	10°♓34'℞
03-27-1993	11°♓17'
04-03-1993	15°♓51'
04-10-1993	23°♓04'
04-17-1993	02°♈11'
04-24-1993	12°♈51'
05-01-1993	24°♈57'
05-08-1993	08°♉28'
05-15-1993	23°♉16'
05-22-1993	08°♊31'
05-29-1993	22°♊47'
06-05-1993	05°♋05'
06-12-1993	15°♋05'
06-19-1993	22°♋34'
06-26-1993	27°♋07'
07-03-1993	28°♋10'℞
07-10-1993	25°♋37'℞
07-17-1993	21°♋12'℞
07-24-1993	18°♋17'℞
07-31-1993	19°♋35'
08-07-1993	25°♋51'
08-14-1993	06°♌29'
08-21-1993	19°♌49'
08-28-1993	03°♍47'
09-04-1993	17°♍08'
09-11-1993	29°♍33'

Sep 18, 1993 00:00 am EST

Date	☿ Geo Lon
09-18-1993	11°♎03'
09-25-1993	21°♎42'
10-02-1993	01°♏30'
10-09-1993	10°♏19'
10-16-1993	17°♏35'
10-23-1993	22°♏03'
10-30-1993	21°♏11'℞
11-06-1993	13°♏39'℞
11-13-1993	06°♏55'℞
11-20-1993	08°♏34'
11-27-1993	16°♏03'
12-04-1993	25°♏48'
12-11-1993	06°♐17'
12-18-1993	17°♐02'
12-25-1993	27°♐55'
01-01-1994	09°♑00'
01-08-1994	20°♑21'
01-15-1994	02°♒00'
01-22-1994	13°♒52'
01-29-1994	25°♒19'
02-05-1994	04°♓25'
02-12-1994	07°♓31'℞
02-19-1994	02°♓41'℞
02-26-1994	25°♒28'℞
03-05-1994	22°♒38'℞
03-12-1994	24°♒55'
03-19-1994	00°♓42'
03-26-1994	08°♓42'
04-02-1994	18°♓18'
04-09-1994	29°♓12'
04-16-1994	11°♈22'
04-23-1994	24°♈47'
04-30-1994	09°♉22'
05-07-1994	24°♉25'
05-14-1994	08°♊31'
05-21-1994	20°♊24'
05-28-1994	29°♊33'
06-04-1994	05°♋40'
06-11-1994	08°♋19'
06-18-1994	07°♋21'℞

Jun 25, 1994 00:00 am EST

Date	☿ Geo Lon
06-25-1994	03°♋45'℞
07-02-1994	00°♋15'℞
07-09-1994	29°♊39'
07-16-1994	03°♋12'
07-23-1994	10°♋53'
07-30-1994	22°♋13'
08-06-1994	06°♌00'
08-13-1994	20°♌25'
08-20-1994	04°♍10'
08-27-1994	16°♍50'
09-03-1994	28°♍26'
09-10-1994	09°♎01'
09-17-1994	18°♎33'
09-24-1994	26°♎49'
10-01-1994	03°♏13'
10-08-1994	06°♏25'
10-15-1994	04°♏10'℞
10-22-1994	26°♎22'℞
10-29-1994	20°♎54'℞
11-05-1994	23°♎51'
11-12-1994	02°♏18'
11-19-1994	12°♏46'
11-26-1994	23°♏44'
12-03-1994	04°♐44'
12-10-1994	15°♐44'
12-17-1994	26°♐44'
12-24-1994	07°♑52'
12-31-1994	19°♑09'
01-07-1995	00°♒27'
01-14-1995	11°♒08'
01-21-1995	19°♒13'
01-28-1995	20°♒49'℞
02-04-1995	14°♒21'℞
02-11-1995	07°♒13'℞
02-18-1995	05°♒51'
02-25-1995	09°♒33'
03-04-1995	16°♒18'
03-11-1995	24°♒55'
03-18-1995	04°♓50'
03-25-1995	15°♓52'

Apr 01, 1995 00:00 am EST

☿

Date	Geo Lon
04-01-1995	27°♓59'
04-08-1995	11°♈14'
04-15-1995	25°♈32'
04-22-1995	10°♉17'
04-29-1995	24°♉05'
05-06-1995	05°♊23'
05-13-1995	13°♊23'
05-20-1995	17°♊40'
05-27-1995	18°♊04'Rx
06-03-1995	15°♊14'Rx
06-10-1995	11°♊31'Rx
06-17-1995	09°♊49'Rx
06-24-1995	11°♊39'
07-01-1995	17°♊10'
07-08-1995	26°♊04'
07-15-1995	07°♋59'
07-22-1995	22°♋07'
07-29-1995	06°♌55'
08-05-1995	21°♌01'
08-12-1995	03°♍55'
08-19-1995	15°♍35'
08-26-1995	26°♍03'
09-02-1995	05°♎16'
09-09-1995	12°♎55'
09-16-1995	18°♎21'
09-23-1995	20°♎09'Rx
09-30-1995	16°♎35'Rx
10-07-1995	08°♎57'Rx
10-14-1995	05°♎00'
10-21-1995	09°♎12'
10-28-1995	18°♎35'
11-04-1995	29°♎44'
11-11-1995	11°♏11'
11-18-1995	22°♏28'
11-25-1995	03°♐34'
12-02-1995	14°♐32'
12-09-1995	25°♐27'
12-16-1995	06°♑21'
12-23-1995	17°♑05'
12-30-1995	26°♑57'

Jan 06, 1996 00:00 am EST

☿

Date	Geo Lon
01-06-1996	03°♒58'
01-13-1996	04°♒06'Rx
01-20-1996	26°♑23'Rx
01-27-1996	19°♑50'Rx
02-03-1996	19°♑58'
02-10-1996	24°♑54'
02-17-1996	02°♒27'
02-24-1996	11°♒33'
03-02-1996	21°♒43'
03-09-1996	02°♓48'
03-16-1996	14°♓49'
03-23-1996	27°♓49'
03-30-1996	11°♈45'
04-06-1996	26°♈08'
04-13-1996	09°♉31'
04-20-1996	20°♉04'
04-27-1996	26°♉35'
05-04-1996	28°♉38'Rx
05-11-1996	26°♉38'Rx
05-18-1996	22°♉40'Rx
05-25-1996	19°♉54'Rx
06-01-1996	20°♉23'
06-08-1996	24°♉24'
06-15-1996	01°♊33'
06-22-1996	11°♊25'
06-29-1996	23°♊48'
07-06-1996	08°♋11'
07-13-1996	23°♋16'
07-20-1996	07°♌40'
07-27-1996	20°♌45'
08-03-1996	02°♍26'
08-10-1996	12°♍44'
08-17-1996	21°♍31'
08-24-1996	28°♍27'
08-31-1996	02°♎44'
09-07-1996	03°♎02'Rx
09-14-1996	28°♍21'Rx
09-21-1996	21°♍24'Rx
09-28-1996	19°♍11'
10-05-1996	24°♍36'

Oct 12, 1996 00:00 am EST

	☿
Date	Geo Lon
10-12-1996	04°♎51'
10-19-1996	16°♎41'
10-26-1996	28°♎36'
11-02-1996	10°♏11'
11-09-1996	21°♏25'
11-16-1996	02°♐21'
11-23-1996	13°♐05'
11-30-1996	23°♐36'
12-07-1996	03°♑44'
12-14-1996	12°♑46'
12-21-1996	18°♑38'
12-28-1996	17°♑22'℞
01-04-1997	08°♑49'℞
01-11-1997	03°♑10'℞
01-18-1997	04°♑45'
01-25-1997	10°♑46'
02-01-1997	19°♑02'
02-08-1997	28°♑31'
02-15-1997	08°≈52'
02-22-1997	19°≈57'
03-01-1997	01°♓50'
03-08-1997	14°♓33'
03-15-1997	28°♓05'
03-22-1997	11°♈59'
03-29-1997	24°♈51'
04-05-1997	04°♉28'
04-12-1997	09°♉15'
04-19-1997	08°♉48'℞
04-26-1997	04°♉44'℞
05-03-1997	00°♉39'℞
05-10-1997	29°♈33'
05-17-1997	02°♉10'
05-24-1997	07°♉58'
05-31-1997	16°♉21'
06-07-1997	26°♉59'
06-14-1997	09°♊42'
06-21-1997	24°♊13'
06-28-1997	09°♋29'
07-05-1997	24°♋07'
07-12-1997	07°♌19'

Jul 19, 1997 00:00 am EST

	☿
Date	Geo Lon
07-19-1997	18°♌56'
07-26-1997	28°♌56'
08-02-1997	07°♍10'
08-09-1997	13°♍11'
08-16-1997	16°♍07'
08-23-1997	14°♍52'℞
08-30-1997	09°♍28'℞
09-06-1997	03°♍46'℞
09-13-1997	03°♍27'
09-20-1997	10°♍03'
09-27-1997	21°♍04'
10-04-1997	03°♎33'
10-11-1997	15°♎58'
10-18-1997	27°♎51'
10-25-1997	09°♏13'
11-01-1997	20°♏09'
11-08-1997	00°♐42'
11-15-1997	10°♐51'
11-22-1997	20°♐23'
11-29-1997	28°♐31'
12-06-1997	03°♑11'
12-13-1997	00°♑34'℞
12-20-1997	21°♐35'℞
12-27-1997	17°♐04'℞
01-03-1998	20°♐00'
01-10-1998	27°♐01'
01-17-1998	05°♑53'
01-24-1998	15°♑44'
01-31-1998	26°♑14'
02-07-1998	07°≈18'
02-14-1998	19°≈00'
02-21-1998	01°♓25'
02-28-1998	14°♓30'
03-07-1998	27°♓52'
03-14-1998	10°♈06'
03-21-1998	18°♈41'
03-28-1998	21°♈29'℞
04-04-1998	18°♈33'℞
04-11-1998	13°♈13'℞
04-18-1998	09°♈59'℞

Apr 25, 1998 00:00 am EST

☿

Date	Geo Lon
04-25-1998	10°♈47'
05-02-1998	15°♈11'
05-09-1998	22°♈20'
05-16-1998	01°♉37'
05-23-1998	12°♉46'
05-30-1998	25°♉43'
06-06-1998	10°♊17'
06-13-1998	25°♊37'
06-20-1998	10°♋22'
06-27-1998	23°♋35'
07-04-1998	05°♌01'
07-11-1998	14°♌35'
07-18-1998	22°♌02'
07-25-1998	26°♌51'
08-01-1998	28°♌13'℞
08-08-1998	25°♌29'℞
08-15-1998	20°♌02'℞
08-22-1998	16°♌09'℞
08-29-1998	17°♌47'
09-05-1998	25°♌30'
09-12-1998	07°♍14'
09-19-1998	20°♍20'
09-26-1998	03°♎14'
10-03-1998	15°♎27'
10-10-1998	26°♎58'
10-17-1998	07°♏53'
10-24-1998	18°♏16'
10-31-1998	28°♏03'
11-07-1998	06°♐58'
11-14-1998	14°♐10'
11-21-1998	17°♐33'
11-28-1998	13°♐41'℞
12-05-1998	04°♐40'℞
12-12-1998	01°♐23'
12-19-1998	05°♐35'
12-26-1998	13°♐30'
01-02-1999	22°♐58'
01-09-1999	03°♑08'
01-16-1999	13°♑46'
01-23-1999	24°♑49'

Jan 30, 1999 00:00 am EST

☿

Date	Geo Lon
01-30-1999	06°♒20'
02-06-1999	18°♒25'
02-13-1999	01°♓02'
02-20-1999	13°♓47'
02-27-1999	25°♓18'
03-06-1999	02°♈45'
03-13-1999	03°♈29'℞
03-20-1999	28°♓22'℞
03-27-1999	22°♓42'℞
04-03-1999	20°♓54'
04-10-1999	23°♓27'
04-17-1999	29°♓16'
04-24-1999	07°♈23'
05-01-1999	17°♈18'
05-08-1999	28°♈48'
05-15-1999	11°♉51'
05-22-1999	26°♉21'
05-29-1999	11°♊40'
06-05-1999	26°♊26'
06-12-1999	09°♋33'
06-19-1999	20°♋38'
06-26-1999	29°♋31'
07-03-1999	05°♌53'
07-10-1999	09°♌11'
07-17-1999	08°♌47'℞
07-24-1999	04°♌58'℞
07-31-1999	00°♌18'℞
08-07-1999	28°♋39'
08-14-1999	02°♌14'
08-21-1999	11°♌00'
08-28-1999	23°♌21'
09-04-1999	07°♍00'
09-11-1999	20°♍22'
09-18-1999	02°♎55'
09-25-1999	14°♎36'
10-02-1999	25°♎32'
10-09-1999	05°♏44'
10-16-1999	15°♏08'
10-23-1999	23°♏24'
10-30-1999	29°♏36'

Nov 06, 1999 00:00 am EST

☿

Date	Geo Lon
11-06-1999	01° ♐ 38' ℞
11-13-1999	26° ♏ 38' ℞
11-20-1999	17° ♏ 57' ℞
11-27-1999	15° ♏ 59'
12-04-1999	21° ♏ 23'
12-11-1999	00° ♐ 10'
12-18-1999	10° ♐ 11'
12-25-1999	20° ♐ 41'
01-01-2000	01° ♑ 26'
01-08-2000	12° ♑ 27'
01-15-2000	23° ♑ 48'
01-22-2000	05° ♒ 33'
01-29-2000	17° ♒ 40'
02-05-2000	29° ♒ 47'
02-12-2000	10° ♓ 29'
02-19-2000	16° ♓ 43'
02-26-2000	15° ♓ 25' ℞
03-04-2000	08° ♓ 40' ℞
03-11-2000	03° ♓ 29' ℞
03-18-2000	03° ♓ 19'
03-25-2000	07° ♓ 22'
04-01-2000	14° ♓ 15'
04-08-2000	23° ♓ 04'
04-15-2000	03° ♈ 23'
04-22-2000	15° ♈ 04'
04-29-2000	28° ♈ 07'
05-06-2000	12° ♉ 29'
05-13-2000	27° ♉ 38'
05-20-2000	12° ♊ 19'
05-27-2000	25° ♊ 13'
06-03-2000	05° ♋ 44'
06-10-2000	13° ♋ 38'
06-17-2000	18° ♋ 32'
06-24-2000	19° ♋ 56' ℞
07-01-2000	17° ♋ 48' ℞
07-08-2000	13° ♋ 39' ℞
07-15-2000	10° ♋ 38' ℞
07-22-2000	11° ♋ 24'
07-29-2000	16° ♋ 48'
08-05-2000	26° ♋ 31'

Aug 12, 2000 00:00 am EST

☿

Date	Geo Lon
08-12-2000	09° ♌ 24'
08-19-2000	23° ♌ 33'
08-26-2000	07° ♍ 22'
09-02-2000	20° ♍ 14'
09-09-2000	02° ♎ 05'
09-16-2000	13° ♎ 00'
09-23-2000	23° ♎ 01'
09-30-2000	02° ♏ 01'
10-07-2000	09° ♏ 34'
10-14-2000	14° ♏ 42'
10-21-2000	15° ♏ 20' ℞
10-28-2000	09° ♏ 22' ℞
11-04-2000	01° ♏ 24' ℞
11-11-2000	00° ♏ 47'
11-18-2000	07° ♏ 18'
11-25-2000	16° ♏ 54'
12-02-2000	27° ♏ 28'
12-09-2000	08° ♐ 17'
12-16-2000	19° ♐ 11'
12-23-2000	00° ♑ 12'
12-30-2000	11° ♑ 22'
01-06-2001	22° ♑ 47'
01-13-2001	04° ♒ 24'
01-20-2001	15° ♒ 50'
01-27-2001	25° ♒ 39'
02-03-2001	00° ♓ 37'
02-10-2001	27° ♒ 25' ℞
02-17-2001	19° ♒ 41' ℞
02-24-2001	15° ♒ 32' ℞
03-03-2001	16° ♒ 57'
03-10-2001	22° ♒ 15'
03-17-2001	29° ♒ 57'
03-24-2001	09° ♓ 15'
03-31-2001	19° ♓ 50'
04-07-2001	01° ♈ 35'
04-14-2001	14° ♈ 32'
04-21-2001	28° ♈ 41'
04-28-2001	13° ♉ 36'
05-05-2001	28° ♉ 04'
05-12-2001	10° ♊ 36'

May 19, 2001 00:00 am EST — ☿

Date	Geo Lon
05-19-2001	20° Ⅱ 19'
05-26-2001	26° Ⅱ 50'
06-02-2001	29° Ⅱ 49'
06-09-2001	29° Ⅱ 05' Rx
06-16-2001	25° Ⅱ 39' Rx
06-23-2001	22° Ⅱ 12' Rx
06-30-2001	21° Ⅱ 25'
07-07-2001	24° Ⅱ 32'
07-14-2001	01° ♋ 32'
07-21-2001	12° ♋ 05'
07-28-2001	25° ♋ 25'
08-04-2001	09° ♌ 59'
08-11-2001	24° ♌ 13'
08-18-2001	07° ♍ 22'
08-25-2001	19° ♍ 23'
09-01-2001	00° ♎ 16'
09-08-2001	10° ♎ 04'
09-15-2001	18° ♎ 35'
09-22-2001	25° ♎ 22'
09-29-2001	29° ♎ 19'
10-06-2001	28° ♎ 29' Rx
10-13-2001	21° ♎ 49' Rx
10-20-2001	14° ♎ 57' Rx
10-27-2001	15° ♎ 44'
11-03-2001	23° ♎ 18'
11-10-2001	03° ♏ 41'
11-17-2001	14° ♏ 47'
11-24-2001	25° ♏ 57'
12-01-2001	07° ♐ 00'
12-08-2001	18° ♐ 00'
12-15-2001	29° ♐ 01'
12-22-2001	10° ♑ 07'
12-29-2001	21° ♑ 13'
01-05-2002	01° ♒ 55'
01-12-2002	10° ♒ 48'
01-19-2002	14° ♒ 28' Rx
01-26-2002	09° ♒ 37' Rx
02-02-2002	01° ♒ 29' Rx
02-09-2002	28° ♑ 39'
02-16-2002	01° ♒ 32'

Feb 23, 2002 00:00 am EST — ☿

Date	Geo Lon
02-23-2002	07° ♒ 52'
03-02-2002	16° ♒ 12'
03-09-2002	25° ♒ 52'
03-16-2002	06° ♓ 36'
03-23-2002	18° ♓ 21'
03-30-2002	01° ♈ 08'
04-06-2002	14° ♈ 58'
04-13-2002	29° ♈ 33'
04-20-2002	13° ♉ 42'
04-27-2002	25° ♉ 43'
05-04-2002	04° Ⅱ 22'
05-11-2002	09° Ⅱ 07'
05-18-2002	09° Ⅱ 45' Rx
05-25-2002	07° Ⅱ 00' Rx
06-01-2002	03° Ⅱ 13' Rx
06-08-2002	01° Ⅱ 22' Rx
06-15-2002	02° Ⅱ 59'
06-22-2002	08° Ⅱ 08'
06-29-2002	16° Ⅱ 29'
07-06-2002	27° Ⅱ 45'
07-13-2002	11° ♋ 25'
07-20-2002	26° ♋ 18'
07-27-2002	10° ♌ 53'
08-03-2002	24° ♌ 18'
08-10-2002	06° ♍ 25'
08-17-2002	17° ♍ 14'
08-24-2002	26° ♍ 45'
08-31-2002	04° ♎ 44'
09-07-2002	10° ♎ 36'
09-14-2002	13° ♎ 13'
09-21-2002	10° ♎ 57' Rx
09-28-2002	03° ♎ 59' Rx
10-05-2002	28° ♍ 33' Rx
10-12-2002	00° ♎ 46'
10-19-2002	09° ♎ 18'
10-26-2002	20° ♎ 26'
11-02-2002	02° ♏ 06'
11-09-2002	13° ♏ 36'
11-16-2002	24° ♏ 50'
11-23-2002	05° ♐ 51'

Nov 30, 2002 00:00 am EST

☿

Date	Geo Lon
11-30-2002	16°♐43'
12-07-2002	27°♐30'
12-14-2002	08°♑06'
12-21-2002	18°♑03'
12-28-2002	25°♑56'
01-04-2003	28°♑16'℞
01-11-2003	22°♑01'℞
01-18-2003	14°♑02'℞
01-25-2003	12°♑36'
02-01-2003	16°♑47'
02-08-2003	24°♑00'
02-15-2003	02°♒53'
02-22-2003	12°♒49'
03-01-2003	23°♒39'
03-08-2003	05°♓19'
03-15-2003	17°♓53'
03-22-2003	01°♈23'
03-29-2003	15°♈32'
04-05-2003	29°♈16'
04-12-2003	10°♉38'
04-19-2003	17°♉58'
04-26-2003	20°♉33'
05-03-2003	18°♉42'℞
05-10-2003	14°♉33'℞
05-17-2003	11°♉29'℞
05-24-2003	11°♉42'
05-31-2003	15°♉28'
06-07-2003	22°♉17'
06-14-2003	01°♊42'
06-21-2003	13°♊30'
06-28-2003	27°♊25'
07-05-2003	12°♋31'
07-12-2003	27°♋22'
07-19-2003	10°♌59'
07-26-2003	23°♌09'
08-02-2003	03°♍50'
08-09-2003	12°♍58'
08-16-2003	20°♍15'
08-23-2003	25°♍03'
08-30-2003	26°♍12'℞

Sep 06, 2003 00:00 am EST

☿

Date	Geo Lon
09-06-2003	22°♍36'℞
09-13-2003	15°♍53'℞
09-20-2003	12°♍12'℞
09-27-2003	15°♍51'
10-04-2003	25°♍18'
10-11-2003	07°♎09'
10-18-2003	19°♎22'
10-25-2003	01°♏14'
11-01-2003	12°♏39'
11-08-2003	23°♏41'
11-15-2003	04°♐25'
11-22-2003	14°♐54'
11-29-2003	24°♐59'
12-06-2003	04°♑11'
12-13-2003	10°♑59'
12-20-2003	11°♑57'℞
12-27-2003	04°♑38'℞
01-03-2004	27°♐10'℞
01-10-2004	27°♐10'
01-17-2004	02°♑32'
01-24-2004	10°♑32'
01-31-2004	19°♑52'
02-07-2004	00°♒02'
02-14-2004	10°♒54'
02-21-2004	22°♒28'
02-28-2004	04°♓47'
03-06-2004	17°♓54'
03-13-2004	01°♈34'
03-20-2004	14°♈46'
03-27-2004	25°♈21'
04-03-2004	01°♉09'
04-10-2004	01°♉19'℞
04-17-2004	27°♈15'℞
04-24-2004	22°♈43'℞
05-01-2004	21°♈08'
05-08-2004	23°♈23'
05-15-2004	28°♈54'
05-22-2004	06°♉59'
05-29-2004	17°♉11'
06-05-2004	29°♉23'

Jun 12, 2004 00:00 am EST

Date	☿ Geo Lon
06-12-2004	13° ♊ 26'
06-19-2004	28° ♊ 39'
06-26-2004	13° ♋ 41'
07-03-2004	27° ♋ 25'
07-10-2004	09° ♌ 32'
07-17-2004	19° ♌ 57'
07-24-2004	28° ♌ 33'
07-31-2004	04° ♍ 57'
08-07-2004	08° ♍ 26'
08-14-2004	07° ♍ 59' ℞
08-21-2004	03° ♍ 24' ℞
08-28-2004	27° ♌ 36' ℞
09-04-2004	25° ♌ 56'
09-11-2004	00° ♍ 59'
09-18-2004	11° ♍ 16'
09-25-2004	23° ♍ 48'
10-02-2004	06° ♎ 33'
10-09-2004	18° ♎ 47'
10-16-2004	00° ♏ 25'
10-23-2004	11° ♏ 29'
10-30-2004	22° ♏ 06'
11-06-2004	02° ♐ 17'
11-13-2004	11° ♐ 51'
11-20-2004	20° ♐ 14'
11-27-2004	25° ♐ 55'
12-04-2004	25° ♐ 32' ℞
12-11-2004	17° ♐ 26' ℞
12-18-2004	10° ♐ 49' ℞
12-25-2004	12° ♐ 11'
01-01-2005	18° ♐ 38'
01-08-2005	27° ♐ 20'
01-15-2005	07° ♑ 06'
01-22-2005	17° ♑ 28'
01-29-2005	28° ♑ 22'
02-05-2005	09° ♒ 48'
02-12-2005	21° ♒ 51'
02-19-2005	04° ♓ 33'
02-26-2005	17° ♓ 40'
03-05-2005	00° ♈ 14'
03-12-2005	09° ♈ 57'

Mar 19, 2005 00:00 am EST

Date	☿ Geo Lon
03-19-2005	14° ♈ 03'
03-26-2005	11° ♈ 46' ℞
04-02-2005	06° ♈ 07' ℞
04-09-2005	02° ♈ 11' ℞
04-16-2005	02° ♈ 23'
04-23-2005	06° ♈ 24'
04-30-2005	13° ♈ 14'
05-07-2005	22° ♈ 12'
05-14-2005	02° ♉ 58'
05-21-2005	15° ♉ 25'
05-28-2005	29° ♉ 30'
06-04-2005	14° ♊ 43'
06-11-2005	29° ♊ 49'
06-18-2005	13° ♋ 36'
06-25-2005	25° ♋ 32'
07-02-2005	05° ♌ 31'
07-09-2005	13° ♌ 21'
07-16-2005	18° ♌ 35'
07-23-2005	20° ♌ 28' ℞
07-30-2005	18° ♌ 25' ℞
08-06-2005	13° ♌ 27' ℞
08-13-2005	09° ♌ 15' ℞
08-20-2005	09° ♌ 46'
08-27-2005	16° ♌ 11'
09-03-2005	27° ♌ 12'
09-10-2005	10° ♍ 21'
09-17-2005	23° ♍ 37'
09-24-2005	06° ♎ 14'
10-01-2005	18° ♎ 05'
10-08-2005	29° ♎ 13'
10-15-2005	09° ♏ 43'
10-22-2005	19° ♏ 35'
10-29-2005	28° ♏ 37'
11-05-2005	06° ♐ 10'
11-12-2005	10° ♐ 38'
11-19-2005	08° ♐ 54' ℞
11-26-2005	00° ♐ 22' ℞
12-03-2005	24° ♏ 49' ℞
12-10-2005	27° ♏ 30'
12-17-2005	04° ♐ 57'

Dec 22, 2005 00:00 am EST		Sep 28, 2006 00:00 am EST	
	☿		☿
Date	Geo Lon	Date	Geo Lon
12-22-2005	11°♐32'	09-28-2006	24°♎19'
12-29-2005	21°♐32'	10-05-2006	04°♏07'
01-05-2006	02°♑00'	10-12-2006	12°♏56'
01-12-2006	12°♑48'	10-19-2006	20°♏13'
01-19-2006	23°♑59'	10-26-2006	24°♏39'
01-26-2006	05°≈37'	11-02-2006	23°♏39'Rx
02-02-2006	17°≈45'	11-09-2006	15°♏55'Rx
02-09-2006	00°♓16'	11-16-2006	09°♏22'Rx
02-16-2006	12°♓30'	11-23-2006	11°♏15'
02-23-2006	22°♓28'	11-30-2006	18°♏46'
03-02-2006	26°♓53'	12-07-2006	28°♏29'
03-09-2006	24°♓02'Rx	12-14-2006	08°♐56'
03-16-2006	17°♓30'Rx	12-21-2006	19°♐38'
03-23-2006	13°♓27'Rx	12-28-2006	00°♑32'
03-30-2006	14°♓09'	01-04-2007	11°♑38'
04-06-2006	18°♓42'	01-11-2007	23°♑01'
04-13-2006	25°♓54'	01-18-2007	04°≈46'
04-20-2006	05°♈01'	01-25-2007	16°≈43'
04-27-2006	15°♈43'	02-01-2007	28°≈13'
05-04-2006	27°♈52'	02-08-2007	07°♓15'
05-11-2006	11°♉29'	02-15-2007	10°♓08'Rx
05-18-2006	26°♉22'	02-22-2007	05°♓15'Rx
05-25-2006	11°♊36'	03-01-2007	28°≈10'Rx
06-01-2006	25°♊48'	03-08-2007	25°≈25'
06-08-2006	08°♋02'	03-15-2007	27°≈43'
06-15-2006	18°♋01'	03-22-2007	03°♓29'
06-22-2006	25°♋32'	03-29-2007	11°♓29'
06-29-2006	00°♌10'	04-05-2007	21°♓06'
07-06-2006	01°♌18'Rx	04-12-2007	02°♈02'
07-13-2006	28°♋48'Rx	04-19-2007	14°♈16'
07-20-2006	24°♋17'Rx	04-26-2007	27°♈46'
07-27-2006	21°♋13'Rx	05-03-2007	12°♉27'
08-03-2006	22°♋27'	05-10-2007	27°♉31'
08-10-2006	28°♋45'	05-17-2007	11°♊33'
08-17-2006	09°♌28'	05-24-2007	23°♊23'
08-24-2006	22°♌49'	05-31-2007	02°♋32'
08-31-2006	06°♍42'	06-07-2007	08°♋42'
09-07-2006	19°♍57'	06-14-2007	11°♋29'
09-14-2006	02°♎16'	06-21-2007	10°♋37'Rx
09-21-2006	13°♎42'	06-28-2007	07°♋02'Rx

Jul 05, 2007 00:00 am EST

Date	☿ Geo Lon
07-05-2007	03°♋25'Rx
07-12-2007	02°♋40'
07-19-2007	06°♋07'
07-26-2007	13°♋50'
08-02-2007	25°♋14'
08-09-2007	09°♌02'
08-16-2007	23°♌23'
08-23-2007	07°♍01'
08-30-2007	19°♍36'
09-06-2007	01°♎07'
09-13-2007	11°♎39'
09-20-2007	21°♎11'
09-27-2007	29°♎27'
10-04-2007	05°♏52'
10-11-2007	09°♏02'
10-18-2007	06°♏38'Rx
10-25-2007	28°♎42'Rx
11-01-2007	23°♎25'Rx
11-08-2007	26°♎34'
11-15-2007	05°♏04'
11-22-2007	15°♏29'
11-29-2007	26°♏23'
12-06-2007	07°♐21'
12-13-2007	18°♐20'
12-20-2007	29°♐22'
12-27-2007	10°♑32'
01-03-2008	21°♑52'
01-10-2008	03°♒15'
01-17-2008	13°♒58'
01-24-2008	21°♒59'
01-31-2008	23°♒21'Rx
02-07-2008	16°♒48'Rx
02-14-2008	09°♒50'Rx
02-21-2008	08°♒34'
02-28-2008	12°♒17'
03-06-2008	19°♒01'
03-13-2008	27°♒38'
03-20-2008	07°♓35'
03-27-2008	18°♓40'
04-03-2008	00°♈51'

Apr 10, 2008 00:00 am EST

Date	☿ Geo Lon
04-10-2008	14°♈11'
04-17-2008	28°♈35'
04-24-2008	13°♉23'
05-01-2008	27°♉08'
05-08-2008	08°♊22'
05-15-2008	16°♊23'
05-22-2008	20°♊46'
05-29-2008	21°♊18'Rx
06-05-2008	18°♊35'Rx
06-12-2008	14°♊51'Rx
06-19-2008	12°♊59'Rx
06-26-2008	14°♊40'
07-03-2008	20°♊07'
07-10-2008	29°♊02'
07-17-2008	11°♋01'
07-24-2008	25°♋10'
07-31-2008	09°♌55'
08-07-2008	23°♌55'
08-14-2008	06°♍43'
08-21-2008	18°♍18'
08-28-2008	28°♍44'
09-04-2008	07°♎56'
09-11-2008	15°♎36'
09-18-2008	21°♎01'
09-25-2008	22°♎47'Rx
10-02-2008	19°♎06'Rx
10-09-2008	11°♎21'Rx
10-16-2008	07°♎35'
10-23-2008	11°♎59'
10-30-2008	21°♎24'
11-06-2008	02°♏30'
11-13-2008	13°♏52'
11-20-2008	25°♏06'
11-27-2008	06°♐10'
12-04-2008	17°♐09'
12-11-2008	28°♐06'
12-18-2008	09°♑03'
12-25-2008	19°♑50'
01-01-2009	29°♑45'
01-08-2009	06°♒40'

Jan 15, 2009 00:00 am EST

Date	☿ Geo Lon
01-15-2009	06°≈33'℞
01-22-2009	28°♑45'℞
01-29-2009	22°♑24'℞
02-05-2009	22°♑38'
02-12-2009	27°♑35'
02-19-2009	05°≈08'
02-26-2009	14°≈14'
03-05-2009	24°≈25'
03-12-2009	05°♓33'
03-19-2009	17°♓38'
03-26-2009	00°♈44'
04-02-2009	14°♈47'
04-09-2009	29°♈13'
04-16-2009	12°♉33'
04-23-2009	23°♉02'
04-30-2009	29°♉34'
05-07-2009	01°♊45'℞
05-14-2009	29°♉54'℞
05-21-2009	26°♉00'℞
05-28-2009	23°♉10'℞
06-04-2009	23°♉31'
06-11-2009	27°♉25'
06-18-2009	04°♊30'
06-25-2009	14°♊24'
07-02-2009	26°♊51'
07-09-2009	11°♋16'
07-16-2009	26°♋18'
07-23-2009	10°♌37'
07-30-2009	23°♌36'
08-06-2009	05°♍13'
08-13-2009	15°♍28'
08-20-2009	24°♍14'
08-27-2009	01°♎11'
09-03-2009	05°♎28'
09-10-2009	05°♎45'℞
09-17-2009	00°♎57'℞
09-24-2009	23°♍55'℞
10-01-2009	21°♍51'
10-08-2009	27°♍27'
10-15-2009	07°♎43'

Oct 22, 2009 00:00 am EST

Date	☿ Geo Lon
10-22-2009	19°♎29'
10-29-2009	01°♏19'
11-05-2009	12°♏50'
11-12-2009	24°♏01'
11-19-2009	04°♐57'
11-26-2009	15°♐42'
12-03-2009	26°♐16'
12-10-2009	06°♑27'
12-17-2009	15°♑31'
12-24-2009	21°♑17'
12-31-2009	19°♑45'℞
01-07-2010	11°♑08'℞
01-14-2010	05°♑43'℞
01-21-2010	07°♑24'
01-28-2010	13°♑27'
02-04-2010	21°♑41'
02-11-2010	01°≈10'
02-18-2010	11°≈32'
02-25-2010	22°≈41'
03-04-2010	04°♓37'
03-11-2010	17°♓25'
03-18-2010	01°♈04'
03-25-2010	15°♈02'
04-01-2010	27°♈52'
04-08-2010	07°♉25'
04-15-2010	12°♉11'
04-22-2010	11°♉52'℞
04-29-2010	07°♉57'℞
05-06-2010	03°♉54'℞
05-13-2010	02°♉43'
05-20-2010	05°♉14'
05-27-2010	10°♉57'
06-03-2010	19°♉18'
06-10-2010	29°♉57'
06-17-2010	12°♊45'
06-24-2010	27°♊20'
07-01-2010	12°♋34'
07-08-2010	27°♋06'
07-15-2010	10°♌13'
07-22-2010	21°♌46'

Jul 29, 2010 00:00 am EST

☿

Date	Geo Lon
07-29-2010	01°♍44'
08-05-2010	09°♍57'
08-12-2010	15°♍59'
08-19-2010	18°♍56'
08-26-2010	17°♍40'Rx
09-02-2010	12°♍10'Rx
09-09-2010	06°♍24'Rx
09-16-2010	06°♍11'
09-23-2010	12°♍56'
09-30-2010	23°♍59'
10-07-2010	06°♎24'
10-14-2010	18°♎42'
10-21-2010	00°♏32'
10-28-2010	11°♏51'
11-04-2010	22°♏45'
11-11-2010	03°♐19'
11-18-2010	13°♐30'
11-25-2010	23°♐05'
12-02-2010	01°♑14'
12-09-2010	05°♑48'
12-16-2010	02°♑55'Rx
12-23-2010	23°♐54'Rx
12-30-2010	19°♐38'Rx
01-06-2011	22°♐40'
01-13-2011	29°♐41'
01-20-2011	08°♑33'
01-27-2011	18°♑23'
02-03-2011	28°♑53'
02-10-2011	10°♒00'
02-17-2011	21°♒46'
02-24-2011	04°♓15'
03-03-2011	17°♓27'
03-10-2011	00°♈53'
03-17-2011	13°♈05'
03-24-2011	21°♈35'
03-31-2011	24°♈21'Rx
04-07-2011	21°♈32'Rx
04-14-2011	16°♈19'Rx
04-21-2011	13°♈06'Rx
04-28-2011	13°♈49'

May 05, 2011 00:00 am EST

☿

Date	Geo Lon
05-05-2011	18°♈09'
05-12-2011	25°♈16'
05-19-2011	04°♉32'
05-26-2011	15°♉44'
06-02-2011	28°♉45'
06-09-2011	13°♊23'
06-16-2011	28°♊43'
06-23-2011	13°♋23'
06-30-2011	26°♋31'
07-07-2011	07°♌54'
07-14-2011	17°♌26'
07-21-2011	24°♌54'
07-28-2011	29°♌45'
08-04-2011	01°♍09'Rx
08-11-2011	28°♌25'Rx
08-18-2011	22°♌51'Rx
08-25-2011	18°♌53'Rx
09-01-2011	20°♌35'
09-08-2011	28°♌26'
09-15-2011	10°♍12'
09-22-2011	23°♍13'
09-29-2011	06°♎01'
10-06-2011	18°♎09'
10-13-2011	29°♎37'
10-20-2011	10°♏30'
10-27-2011	20°♏52'
11-03-2011	00°♐41'
11-10-2011	09°♐38'
11-17-2011	16°♐50'
11-24-2011	20°♐07'
12-01-2011	15°♐59'Rx
12-08-2011	06°♐59'Rx
12-15-2011	03°♐58'
12-22-2011	08°♐16'
12-29-2011	16°♐11'
01-05-2012	25°♐37'
01-12-2012	05°♑46'
01-19-2012	16°♑24'
01-26-2012	27°♑29'
02-02-2012	09°♒04'

Feb 09, 2012 00:00 am EST	
	☿
Date	Geo Lon
02-09-2012	21°≈13'
02-16-2012	03°♓56'
02-23-2012	16°♓46'
03-01-2012	28°♓15'
03-08-2012	05°♈35'
03-15-2012	06°♈14'Rx
03-22-2012	01°♈13'Rx
03-29-2012	25°♓39'Rx
04-05-2012	23°♓53'
04-12-2012	26°♓23'
04-19-2012	02°♈09'
04-26-2012	10°♈16'
05-03-2012	20°♈11'
05-10-2012	01°♉44'
05-17-2012	14°♉51'
05-24-2012	29°♉26'
05-31-2012	14°♊46'
06-07-2012	29°♊29'
06-14-2012	12°♋31'
06-21-2012	23°♋33'
06-28-2012	02°♌26'
07-05-2012	08°♌51'
07-12-2012	12°♌13'
07-19-2012	11°♌52'Rx
07-26-2012	08°♌02'Rx
08-02-2012	03°♌14'Rx
08-09-2012	01°♌29'
08-16-2012	05°♌05'
08-23-2012	13°♌57'
08-30-2012	26°♌21'
09-06-2012	09°♍56'
09-13-2012	23°♍12'
09-20-2012	05°♎39'
09-27-2012	17°♎16'
10-04-2012	28°♎09'
10-11-2012	08°♏21'
10-18-2012	17°♏46'
10-25-2012	26°♏03'
11-01-2012	02°♐15'
11-08-2012	04°♐11'Rx

Nov 15, 2012 00:00 am EST	
	☿
Date	Geo Lon
11-15-2012	28°♏56'Rx
11-22-2012	20°♏18'Rx
11-29-2012	18°♏36'
12-06-2012	24°♏06'
12-13-2012	02°♐52'
12-20-2012	12°♐51'
12-27-2012	23°♐18'
01-03-2013	04°♑04'
01-10-2013	15°♑06'
01-17-2013	26°♑30'
01-24-2013	08°≈19'
01-31-2013	20°≈32'
02-07-2013	02°♓42'
02-14-2013	13°♓24'
02-21-2013	19°♓28'
02-28-2013	18°♓03'Rx
03-07-2013	11°♓23'Rx
03-14-2013	06°♓19'Rx
03-21-2013	06°♓11'
03-28-2013	10°♓12'
04-04-2013	17°♓04'
04-11-2013	25°♓53'
04-18-2013	06°♈14'
04-25-2013	17°♈58'
05-02-2013	01°♉06'
05-09-2013	15°♉33'
05-16-2013	00°♊45'
05-23-2013	15°♊23'
05-30-2013	28°♊13'
06-06-2013	08°♋42'
06-13-2013	16°♋37'
06-20-2013	21°♋35'
06-27-2013	23°♋06'Rx
07-04-2013	21°♋01'Rx
07-11-2013	16°♋49'Rx
07-18-2013	13°♋39'Rx
07-25-2013	14°♋18'
08-01-2013	19°♋42'
08-08-2013	29°♋30'
08-15-2013	12°♌26'

Aug 22, 2013 00:00 am EST ☿

Date	Geo Lon
08-22-2013	26° ♌32'
08-29-2013	10° ♍14'
09-05-2013	23° ♍00'
09-12-2013	04° ♎47'
09-19-2013	15° ♎39'
09-26-2013	25° ♎39'
10-03-2013	04° ♏39'
10-10-2013	12° ♏13'
10-17-2013	17° ♏21'
10-24-2013	17° ♏52'℞
10-31-2013	11° ♏41'℞
11-07-2013	03° ♏47'℞
11-14-2013	03° ♏27'
11-21-2013	10° ♏04'
11-28-2013	19° ♏38'
12-05-2013	00° ♐09'
12-12-2013	10° ♐56'
12-19-2013	21° ♐49'
12-26-2013	02° ♑49'
01-02-2014	14° ♑02'
01-09-2014	25° ♑31'
01-16-2014	07° ♒13'
01-23-2014	18° ♒42'
01-30-2014	28° ♒30'
02-06-2014	03° ♓18'
02-13-2014	29° ♒56'℞
02-20-2014	22° ♒18'℞
02-27-2014	18° ♒16'℞
03-06-2014	19° ♒44'
03-13-2014	25° ♒01'
03-20-2014	02° ♓42'
03-27-2014	12° ♓01'
04-03-2014	22° ♓39'
04-10-2014	04° ♈27'
04-17-2014	17° ♈30'
04-24-2014	01° ♉44'
05-01-2014	16° ♉42'
05-08-2014	01° ♊09'
05-15-2014	13° ♊36'
05-22-2014	23° ♊18'

May 29, 2014 00:00 am EST ☿

Date	Geo Lon
05-29-2014	29° ♊53'
06-05-2014	02° ♋58'
06-12-2014	02° ♋22'℞
06-19-2014	29° ♊00'℞
06-26-2014	25° ♊26'℞
07-03-2014	24° ♊30'
07-10-2014	27° ♊29'
07-17-2014	04° ♋29'
07-24-2014	15° ♋06'
07-31-2014	28° ♋29'
08-07-2014	13° ♌01'
08-14-2014	27° ♌08'
08-21-2014	10° ♍11'
08-28-2014	22° ♍06'
09-04-2014	02° ♎57'
09-11-2014	12° ♎43'
09-18-2014	21° ♎15'
09-25-2014	28° ♎02'
10-02-2014	01° ♏58'
10-09-2014	01° ♏02'℞
10-16-2014	24° ♎12'℞
10-23-2014	17° ♎24'℞
10-30-2014	18° ♎27'
11-06-2014	26° ♎06'
11-13-2014	06° ♏26'
11-20-2014	17° ♏29'
11-27-2014	28° ♏35'
12-04-2014	09° ♐37'
12-11-2014	20° ♐37'
12-18-2014	01° ♑39'
12-25-2014	12° ♑48'
01-01-2015	23° ♑59'
01-08-2015	04° ♒45'
01-15-2015	13° ♒36'
01-22-2015	17° ♒04'℞
01-29-2015	12° ♒01'℞
02-05-2015	04° ♒01'℞
02-12-2015	01° ♒19'
02-19-2015	04° ♒14'
02-26-2015	10° ♒34'

Mar 05, 2015 00:00 am EST

Date	☿ Geo Lon
03-05-2015	18°♒55'
03-12-2015	28°♒36'
03-19-2015	09°♓22'
03-26-2015	21°♓10'
04-02-2015	04°♈03'
04-09-2015	17°♈59'
04-16-2015	02°♉38'
04-23-2015	16°♉47'
04-30-2015	28°♉44'
05-07-2015	07°♊22'
05-14-2015	12°♊11'
05-21-2015	12°♊58'℞
05-28-2015	10°♊21'℞
06-04-2015	06°♊34'℞
06-11-2015	04°♊35'℞
06-18-2015	06°♊03'
06-25-2015	11°♊07'
07-02-2015	19°♊27'
07-09-2015	00°♋46'
07-16-2015	14°♋30'
07-23-2015	29°♋22'
07-30-2015	13°♌50'
08-06-2015	27°♌09'
08-13-2015	09°♍11'
08-20-2015	19°♍57'
08-27-2015	29°♍26'
09-03-2015	07°♎25'
09-10-2015	13°♎18'
09-17-2015	15°♎54'
09-24-2015	13°♎33'℞
10-01-2015	06°♎27'℞
10-08-2015	01°♎05'℞
10-15-2015	03°♎31'
10-22-2015	12°♎09'
10-29-2015	23°♎14'
11-05-2015	04°♏49'
11-12-2015	16°♏16'
11-19-2015	27°♏27'
11-26-2015	08°♐27'
12-03-2015	19°♐20'

Dec 10, 2015 00:00 am EST

Date	☿ Geo Lon
12-10-2015	00°♑09'
12-17-2015	10°♑49'
12-24-2015	20°♑50'
12-31-2015	28°♑40'

ANALYSIS WORKSHEET

The following worksheet is to be used merely to see how a person perceives and communicates. It is not to be used as a diagnostic tool for the detection of learning disabilities. It is an invaluable insight into the subject's interaction with others, communication skills, perception etc., even when no learning disability is present or suspected.

Fill in the blanks utilizing the information found in the book.

NAME:_____

BIRTH DATE:_____

PLACE OF BIRTH:_____

TIME:_____

Astrological sign for Sun:_____

Astrological sign for Mercury:_____

Sun and Mercury in (select one) same sign   different sign

Influence:_____

_____

_____

Mercury is in the Quality of: (select one) Cardinal Fixed Mutable

Influence:_____

_____

_____

Mercury is in the Element of: (select one)   Fire   Earth   Air   Water

Influence:_____

_____

_____

Mercury is in the _____ House.   Intercepted? (yes   no)

Influence:_____

_____

_____

The Moon is: (select one)   Fast   Slow

A: Perception is:_____

_____

_____

B: Mercury is: (select one) ahead of, or behind, the Sun. Influence:___

_____

_____

C: Combined influence of Sun, Moon and Mercury:

_____

_____

_____

Mercury is Retrograde: (select one) yes no

Influence:_____

_____

_____

Mercury is: (select one)   Casimi   Combust

Influence:_____

_____

_____

Mercury is Conjunct the Planet _____

Influence:_____

_____

_____

List additional aspects to Mercury and their influences:

_____

_____

_____

_____

_____

_____

_____

_____

_____

ANALYSIS WORKSHEET

The following worksheet is to be used merely to see how a person perceives and communicates. It is not to be used as a diagnostic tool for the detection of learning disabilities. It is an invaluable insight into the subject's interaction with others, communication skills, perception etc., even when no learning disability is present or suspected.

Fill in the blanks utilizing the information found in the book.

NAME:_____

BIRTH DATE:_____

PLACE OF BIRTH:_____

TIME:_____

Astrological sign for Sun:_____

Astrological sign for Mercury:_____

Sun and Mercury in (select one) same sign   different sign

Influence:_____

_____

_____

Mercury is in the Quality of: (select one) Cardinal Fixed Mutable

Influence:_____

_____

_____

Mercury is in the Element of: (select one) Fire   Earth   Air   Water

Influence:_____

_____

_____

Mercury is in the _____ House.   Intercepted? (yes   no)

Influence:_____

_____

_____

The Moon is: (select one)   Fast   Slow

A: Perception is:_____

_____

_____

B: Mercury is: (select one) ahead of, or   behind, the Sun.

Influence:_____

_____

_____

C: Combined influence of Sun, Moon and Mercury:

_____

_____

_____

Mercury is Retrograde: (select one) yes no

Influence:_____

_____

_____

Mercury is: (select one)   Casimi   Combust

Influence:_____

_____

_____

Mercury is Conjunct the Planet _____

Influence:_____

_____

_____

List additional aspects to Mercury and their influences:

_____

_____

_____

_____

_____

To order natal and/or progressed charts use the order form below. Enclose a check or money order for $6.00 <u>per chart</u>, payable to *IAM*. Send to IAM, 655 North Queens Avenue, Lindenhurst, NY 11755.

Person placing order: Total Enclosed $ _____

Name: __ _____

Address: _____

City: _____   State: ____   Zip: _____

Phone: (____) _____

Natal ____   Progressed _____

Name _____

Birth Date (mo.)_____   (day)_____   (yr.)_____

Birth Place (city)_____   (state)____   (country)____

Birth Time _____   circle one AM   PM UNKNOWN

Natal ____   Progressed _____

Name _____

Birth Date (mo.)_____   (day)_____   (yr.)_____

Birth Place (city)_____   (state)____   (country)____

Birth Time _____   circle one AM   PM UNKNOWN

Natal ____   Progressed _____

Name _____

Birth Date (mo.)_____   (day)_____   (yr.)_____

Birth Place (city)_____   (state)____   (country)____

Birth Time _____   circle one AM   PM UNKNOWN